'Simply wonderful.'

– BEN FOGLE

'Kate's book has the warmth and calming effect of a log fire and a glass of wine. Unknit your brow and let go. It's a treat.'

– GARETH MALONE

'Kate Humble pours her enviable knowledge into attainable goals. It's a winning combination and the prize – a life in balance with nature – is definitely worth claiming.'

– LUCY SIEGLE

'As ever, where Kate leads, I follow. She has made me reassess and reset.'

– DAN SNOW

Praise for *Thinking On My Feet*

'A lovely, civilized and transporting read, that should have all of us stepping out to meet the world with fresh eyes.'

—HUGH FEARNLEY-WHITTINGSTALL

'An enticing read that makes every walk Humble describes an adventure'

—RANULPH FIENNES

'A beautiful and magnificent book. A paean to a simple act. I defy you to read this book and not be inspired to walk, march or hike – and as a result live a better life more connected with nature and the world around you.'

—SIMON REEVE

'A lovely book, fast-flowing yet at every turn giving the reader pause for thought. Kate Humble makes a delightful companion, her words full of sunshine and the raw pleasure she radiates as she encounters life in its many unexpected forms.'

—BENEDICT ALLEN

Kate Humble

A Year of Living Simply

THE JOYS OF A
LIFE LESS COMPLICATED

aster

Hello. If you've picked up this book in the hope that it will give advice on how to live in a hollow tree, forage for worms and knit a blanket out of leaves, then I'm afraid it won't help you. I'm not sure what will. Maybe you should just go ahead and try living like that. If you like it, carry on. And if you don't, stop. But if you still want to find a way to live more simply that is, perhaps, a bit more attainable, then you could pick up this book again.

Contents

First published in Great Britain in 2020 by Aster, an imprint of
Octopus Publishing Group Ltd
Carmelite House, 50 Victoria Embankment, London EC4Y 0DZ
www.octopusbooks.co.uk
www.octopusbooksusa.com

An Hachette UK Company
www.hachette.co.uk

ISBN 978-1-78325-342-5

A CIP catalogue record for this book is available from the British Library.

Printed and bound in Great Britain

10 9 8 7 6 5 4 3 2 1

Publishing Director: Stephanie Jackson
Creative Director: Jonathan Christie
Senior Editor: Alex Stetter
Production Controller: Lisa Pinell
Illustrations: Beth Marsden

FOR CLARE AND SAM

The Starting Point

WHY SIMPLY?
*

It's been a --- year. I'm not sure of the word to use here. There doesn't seem to be one, or if there is, I don't know it. Perhaps if I just give you the facts, you can fill in the gap for me.

In the first few weeks of this year a number of people I love have died. Jennifer, the beautiful, graceful, infinitely kind woman who took us under her wing when we first moved to Wales and made us part of her family. My father-in-law, with breathtaking suddenness. Di, the dear mum of dear friends. My own dad.

None of these deaths was a tragedy. All had lived into their eighties – my father-in-law was ninety. And all had died with the people they loved beside them, knowing that their lives had mattered, that they would not be forgotten, that they, too, were loved. But I am left now with a tangle of emotions that I can't describe, and I can't put a word to.

And perhaps these losses have helped bring something else into focus, that has, for some time now, been niggling away on the periphery of my thoughts. It's not unpleasant; not one of those vaguely discomforting feelings you get when you might have forgotten something important, or done something that has caused upset, but you're not sure what.

This is more of a quietly forming and growing realization – maybe consciousness is the right word – that life – my life – could be lived differently – more simply – and that I might be happier for it.

I should state right now that I am not unhappy. I'm sad that people I love are no longer around, but not generally unhappy. If life is the lottery some think it is, this particular game of chance has been very benevolent towards me. And it is easy, when life is like mine, with its mix of ups and downs, worries and joys, but nothing too extreme or too challenging, to coast along, content with how things have panned out, slightly of the mind that fate will always be kind. But with the sharp reminders I've had that life is finite, the urge to find a way of living that is more fulfilling has become stronger and more insistent.

And there is another factor at play. The state of the planet that is our home, that sustains all living things, has never been so fragile. It worries me profoundly that the things we do, or don't do, the way of life we have become so used to, that we take for granted, really is no longer tenable. As the late scientist and philosopher Buckminster Fuller observed, 'we are all astronauts on a little spaceship called Earth', but we are a crew in mutiny.

It seems to be an intrinsic factor of human nature to resist change, even when we know that change may be the very thing we need to embrace. How many people do we know that are miserable at work or hate where they live? That are in unhappy relationships or trapped in financial doldrums? How many of us feel a sort of hopelessness when we hear about another great environmental catastrophe? When the headlines are dominated by news of droughts, landslides, devastating storms? When another animal is declared extinct? And how many of us dream about the possibility of a different sort of life?

But change is daunting and difficult. There is no guidebook or helpdesk or blueprint for guaranteed success. Identifying a desire to change is one thing, actually getting started is another challenge altogether. For me it feels like standing at a junction of tracks with signposts pointing in every direction, but with no indication of where they would lead me. So I've done what I often do when I want to try and solve a conundrum. I've opened my notebook, picked up a pen and written a question:

'What would I change?'

And then I've crossed it out. I've scribbled the sort of artless doodle of someone who isn't very good at drawing trying to think. I've penned another question:

'Why change?'

And in answer I've written:

* Life feels more complicated than it needs to be
* To have less financial pressure
* To have more time to walk/read/see friends/learn things
* To have less dependency on others to make/fix stuff
* To have more time for garden/veg bed/animals and be more self-sufficient
* To use less resources and reduce impact on environment
* To counter our throw-away culture and needless waste
* Because I don't want to regret I didn't give it a go.

It's not a plan, as such, but it has given me a sense of where to start. And now in that same notebook is a growing list of things that I want to try to achieve and find out more about. I'm not expecting that by the end of the year I will have come up with a beautifully neat, one-size-fits-all solution. Right at this moment I feel as I do when I'm about to undertake a journey to somewhere I've never been before and the map I'm using is sketchy and vague. There are lots of questions and 'what ifs'. There's the exciting discomfort of uncertainty. I'm sure there will be futile leads, disappointment and failures, as there are on any journey, but I hope there will also be moments of revelation, enlightenment and achievement.

I know I have to be open-minded and always let curiosity get the better of me. I also know I have to be scrupulously honest with myself and accept that some things may not be possible to sustain or won't feel right for me. And most importantly I don't want to run away from real life, to go and be a hermit in a cave, or a wandering monk living on the charity of others. This isn't about living a life of penury, devoid of joy or fun – quite the opposite. It is about finding, or rediscovering, the aspects of life that really matter and having time to value and enjoy them. It is a search for simplicity and the contentment that goes with it.

> *If you have built castles in the air, your work need not be lost;*
> *that is where they should be. Now put foundations under them.*
> HENRY DAVID THOREAU, *WALDEN*

CABIN LIFE
*

It's Sunday evening. I'm sitting in a room full of books and well-worn furniture. There's a big, cast-iron woodburner and baskets full of twigs, logs and old newspapers. There are maps on the wall, several pairs of wellington boots by the door. There's a wonky pile of board games and jigsaw puzzles propped up in one corner, a sheep skull, fossils and the vertebrae of a whale. The view outside the windows that make up most of one wall is dominated by trees, a leafy mosaic of greens, blocking out all but a slither of darkening blue sky. I've wedged the door open with one of the wellies and the only sound is the whispering rustle of leaves and the bleating of sheep somewhere on the hill behind me.

My friend Martha has been coming here since the 60s. Her parents bought two fields and a tumbledown stone house in this still remote, steep-sided valley in mid-Wales. Their plan was to fix up the stone cottage over time, but the neighbouring farmer wouldn't give them access to water or let them tap into his electricity supply, so it remained untouched and instead the family would camp in the field below it every summer. It must have been idyllic in lots of ways. There's a stream at the bottom of the field perfect for paddling, trees to climb and the huge, beckoning expanse of the hills to explore. But the summer weather wasn't always benevolent. Martha remembers a year when the rain and wind were so violent, her canvas tent first collapsed then blew away, leaving her and her sister in a sodden huddle on the groundsheet.

Martha's parents, unable to restore their stone cottage but feeling they needed something a bit more robust and weatherproof for their family to spend their summers in, ordered a flat-packed A-frame house from Sweden and it took two men just two weeks to assemble it. It looks like a giant wooden tent, its tall apex roof sloping down to the ground on each side. There are windows front and back, an open-plan ground floor and a wooden ladder up to another floor where everyone would sleep. It is homely, comforting and gloriously low tech. It does now have electricity and water, but there's no TV, no internet and the signal on my phone disappeared 3 miles down the road. 'I'm away with no access to email or phone messages' my out of office states. I've got five days here. Five days with no timetable and nothing to do other than read, write, walk and think. It is a great luxury. The luxury of simplicity.

And now it's my final night. The woodburner is lit, the dog asleep, stretched out on the wooden floor, my wine glass almost empty. Beyond the windows it is deeply dark and still. A tawny owl calls. A half moon is setting behind the hill. And I sit, my feet in woollen socks resting on the table in front of the warmth of the fire, thinking over the last few days.

On the first morning I woke with the light soon after six, cleaned my teeth, splashed water on my face, pulled on jeans and jumper. I gathered up a map, shoved my feet into boots and, with Teg the dog bounding ahead, went to explore our patch. I followed a narrow sheep track running parallel to the stream, pausing at the edge of the field to look back at the house. It sits well in this landscape. I admired the geometry of it, plain and practical against its backdrop of green. The path soon brought us to a farm track. The map seemed to indicate that the way ahead was a footpath, but there was no sign on the gate to confirm whether it was a right of way. It looked well-used though, so I decided to take it.

In a few moments we were out on the open hill, the land rising steeply to a ridge on our left and the glory of space and sky. It's daunting though.

We're so used to being channelled, guided where to go, whether we are following marked footpaths, road signs or the nagging voice of a satnav. But here it's just me and my dog, my rather shaky navigation skills and the faintest of tracks leading through the heather, that may or may not go anywhere.

I decide I can't go far wrong if I stay roughly on the contour I'm on now, and if I'm on the path that is on the map, we'll meet another that will take me up to the brow of the hill. I'm soon waist-high in bracken, although the path is still clear and definite beneath my feet. Teg disappears, swallowed up by the towering foliage. I push my way through, making for what looks like clear ground ahead. Teg is already there. She relishes this terrain. For the last couple of months, she has been part of a team of dogs gathering sheep and cattle off the slopes of the Brecon Beacons. It's a job for dogs born to be in the mountains – sure-footed and with endless stamina. She waits for me to emerge, then trots ahead on the track that gets fainter and fainter and finally peters out altogether.

Right, I think, *bugger it, let's just head up.* The ground is covered in a thick mat of bilberry and it makes for tricky walking. Teg bounds delightedly through it while I wade inelegantly, panting. The sun has risen above the hills, spilling its soft warm light on the ground. I keep climbing, the bilberry giving way to heather, which is even harder to walk through, but beautiful, vibrant purple glowing in the early sun. I stumble out onto a broad track and as I do so I feel my phone, which I'd put in my pocket, buzz. There's signal up here and I look with dismay as the emails ping through and see that there are some that I really need to address. But there's an advantage to this technological intrusion. I have OS maps on my phone so can check exactly where I am. The little red arrow shows that if I head east along the track I've found, I'll meet another heading north that will bring me in a neat circle back to the house.

Feeling a little bit pleased with myself, I think I'll be even smarter and download the map so I can use it offline. Except that I don't really know how to do it and end up somehow losing the map altogether with no way I can find of getting it back. The paper map I've brought from the house has been much used. There are rips along some of the folds and crucial bits (like the path I'm on now) that have faded and been rubbed away. So instead I look at the landscape. The visibility is breathtaking; I can see for miles. The dark outline of the Brecon Beacons dominates the western skyline. To the north is the opposite slope of this valley. Unlike the rough, uncultivated pasture on this side, it is a patchwork of fields, hedges and coppices, its south-facing ground benefitting from the sun. I make a note of the farms, using them as landmarks so I can gauge roughly where I am in relation to the house, hidden from view, tucked into the slope at the bottom of the hill where I stand.

And quickly a routine establishes itself. I feed Teg, make breakfast for myself, settle down to write or read with a big mug of tea at my side. Teg sleeps, or potters contentedly about in the field outside the house. We go out again in the afternoon, try another route on the other side of the valley, get lost, find our way back. I write again until it gets dark, heat up some soup, stoke the fire, sit with a glass of wine in the company of peace, silence and a sleeping dog.

This morning, out on the hill, I realize that I no longer need the map or worry about where I am. I've taken a different route each morning, feeling increasingly familiar with the landscape and the features that have become the waymarks by which I navigate: the rocky outcrops, the lone tree, the dried-up pond. There has been the odd squally shower some afternoons, but the mornings have always been bright and clear.

Today I climbed up over the ridge and down the south side towards a big pond, its shimmering water rippling in the keen breeze and reflecting the blue of the sky. The air is cold, my fingers tingle with the chill of it, but the sun is warm on my cheek. As I near the pond, a flush of ducks takes flight, circles, leaving behind three chestnut-plumed mergansers to keep watch. A herd of Welsh ponies, grey and chestnut, manes and tails fanned by the wind, regards me warily. They trot away up an incline, then stop and turn their heads, ears pricked, nostrils flaring. As I make my way back up the slope to the ridgeline, I watch two ravens hang motionless in the air, wings spread, silhouetted against the blue of the sky. They are so perfectly still that for a fleeting moment I wonder if they are real, but then they dip and swoop and soar away, riding the thermals, defying gravity.

And now I sit, toasting my toes, reflective. Could I live this pared-down version of life long term? It is so, so tempting to think it possible.

Henry David Thoreau, the American author, philosopher and naturalist, lived in a cabin he built himself for two years and two months. He documented his experiences in his book *Walden*, which has become something of a seminal text on simple living. In March 1845 he borrowed an axe and started to cut the trees that he would use to make the frame of his house. For $4.25 he bought a shack from a man called James Collins and dismantled it so he could re-use the boards that formed the roof, walls and floor for his own. He dug a cellar to store potatoes, erected a frame from the trees he'd cut, covered the frame with the boards he'd bought, and moved in at the beginning of

July. The finished cabin was 10 feet wide and 15 feet long and cost him the grand total of $28.

He survived by growing some of his own food, foraging and fishing and claimed that 'I maintained myself thus solely by the labour of my hands and found that, by working about six weeks a year, I could meet all the expenses of living.'

I laughed when I read this, because it reminded me of something Geoff told me.

Geoff has a beautiful camp in the Flinders Ranges in South Australia. Remote, off-grid, the guests who stay there are drawn by its tranquillity, the beautiful walks, the wildlife and an unparalleled night sky. Geoff's wife does the cooking, while he acts as guide as well as doing all the maintenance of the camp. They love it, but it is a full-time job and they work every day of the week. His nearest neighbour, Adam, is an Aboriginal man and he and Geoff have become great friends over the years.

'But one thing I'll never understand about white folk,' his neighbour said to him one day, over a beer at the camp, 'is that you work so hard just to take two weeks off a year. While I work hard for two weeks so I can have the rest of the year off. Who's got the better life?!'

When Thoreau wasn't working or gathering food, he filled his days writing, thinking and walking for mile after mile through the hills and woods surrounding his cabin. 'We need the tonic of wildness,' he wrote. 'To wade sometimes in the marshes where the bittern and meadow-hen lurk, and hear the booming of the snipe, to smell the whispering sedge where only some wilder and more solitary fowl builds her nest, and the mink crawls with its belly close to the ground...We can never have enough of nature.'

He referred to his time living in the cabin as 'an experiment', to demonstrate to himself, and others, that it was possible to live happily and comfortably without the need to work day in, day out, in order to pay for costly trappings that there was never time to enjoy. It's unclear why he stopped living at Walden and returned to live more conventionally, but he wrote before he left, 'I am convinced, both by faith and experience, that to maintain one's self on this earth is not a hardship, but a pastime, if we live simply and wisely.'

Some years ago, I was making a series of documentaries that involved me being away from home for weeks at a time. The work was fascinating but exhausting, and any day that we weren't filming we were travelling. Television crews don't travel light and every journey we made involved endless manhandling of heavy boxes, wrangles at customs, queues, interminable waits at airports, packing, unpacking, late nights or early mornings. At short notice, the chance came for a break – just a week. And we found somewhere that was the perfect antidote to the hectic pace of life I'd been living: an off-grid cabin beside a lake in rural France. And by happy coincidence it was available the week we wanted. We booked and paid and then I became overwhelmed with doubts. What if the photos had lied, given the impression that it was on its own, when actually there were cabins all around the lake, and jet skis and motorboats and people?

'Well, we can't do anything about it now,' was my husband Ludo's slightly unsympathetic response.

I cheered up when Di, the owner of the cabin, emailed to say it was quite hard to find and suggested we meet her in the car park of the nearest village so we could follow her there. She led us out of the village, down a narrow lane that wound its way through a forest of sweet chestnut trees, then down an even narrower lane, and finally turned onto a rutted dirt track that made its way downhill between ancient oak trees. The track petered out at the lake edge, just beside a small wooden cabin, built on a deck with a jetty leading out over the water and a handmade raft tied to the end. And that was it. There were no other buildings, nothing at all. Just a lake, trees and splendid isolation.

It was a perfect week. We walked, we swam, we read books. We made short forays to local villages for crisp baguettes and smelly cheese. We paddled the raft, cooked on a fire, drank wine. Talked. Laughed. And on our last evening, when Di and her husband Bob came to check everything had been OK, we told them, quite truthfully, that it had been the best holiday we had ever had. 'We've been having cabin fantasies,' I laughed.

Actually, I've been having cabin fantasies for years. I bought Ludo a book when I was working in Canada called *How to Build a Log Cabin*. I don't think he's ever looked at it, but a girl can dream. Bob, though, gave me a questioning look.

'Are you serious?'

'Oh, you know...' I said, a bit embarrassed, 'it's probably like a holiday romance. I'll get over it!'

'It's just that we know of a lake for sale,' Bob continued, 'and it has a sort of fishing hut that goes with it...'

My heart was racing.

'Do you want to go and see it? It's only a few kilometres away.'

We were leaving at five the next morning and hadn't packed.

I looked at Ludo, who raised his eyebrows.

'Of course we do!'

Our little lakeside cabin has become our retreat, a place of respite and rejuvenation. Bob turned the not-very-lovely fishing hut into a thing of beauty. Using wood from trees on our land and on his, he built a staircase and a sleeping platform under the eaves. He panelled the walls, crafted a tiny kitchen, built a deck and roofed it with hand-cut chestnut tiles. It is not much bigger than Thoreau's – about 12 feet by 18 feet. There is no electricity or mains water. Solar panels provide light and power a pump that brings water from the lake to the shower. There's a composting loo, a woodburner, and a small fridge and cooker that run on a gas bottle.

Like Martha's A-frame, there is no TV or internet and our phones get a signal occasionally, but only outside and if we stand in the right spot. Last summer we spent a month there and at the end of it I found it really hard to adjust to 'real life'. We'd talked a lot over that month about the possibility of living there full time and what adjustments or additions we'd need to make for it to work. It's easy being there when the weather is good, because we spend almost all our time outdoors – we even sleep outside on hot nights. We swim in the lake, rarely wear shoes or much in the way of clothes, eat food cooked on the fire.

But when it's wet, or on short winter days, and we are inside more, that's when we notice that there isn't really enough light, that there's no space to hang wet clothes, that two people and three dogs feel like a crowd.

We concluded that what we would need to make it habitable full time was two more rooms – a boot room, for outdoor clothes and wet dogs, and another room besides the one where we cook and eat and sit now – somewhere we can work or just have our own space if we want to. Then we talked about the issue of drinking water – there isn't any: we go to the nearest village and fill up our jerry cans from a tap there. The fact that the kitchen sink (it's actually a caravan sink) is annoyingly small. That if we want hot water, we have to boil the kettle. That if we need to wash clothes, we have to go to the machine outside the supermarket, which is 7 miles away. 'We could wash our clothes by hand,' I suggest, not overly confidently.

I'd been reading a book my friend Phil gave me called *The Plain Reader: Essays on Making a Simple Life*. It is collected writings from an Amish/Quaker/Luddite (as its editor describes it) magazine called *Plain*. My favourite is one entitled 'Hand-Washing Your Clothes' by Brenda Bayles. 'The thought of having to do laundry by hand strikes terror into the hearts of launderers everywhere,' is her opening gambit – how right you are, Brenda! – but, she goes on to say, 'everyone should know how to hand-wash their clothes. To depend on any machine to take care of a basic need is foolhardy.' She claims she can wash an automatic-washer-size load in ten minutes, hang it on the line in five. How does she do it? 'Soaking!' she tells her non-Amish/Quaker/ somewhat Luddite reader, who by now is hooked. Here's Brenda's guide to no-stress laundry:

1. *Fill two tubs with water, one for washing and one for rinsing.*
2. *Add bleach (or biodegradable hydrogen peroxide) and soap to the washtub if needed.* (Brenda is not a fan of soap unless clothes are particular filthy. Otherwise, she says, soaking does the job. And before you say 'But won't everything just smell nasty?' she has an answer for that too. Once soaked, they'll be clean and if you dry them in fresh air and sunshine on a clothes line, 'the clothes smell as clean as they are'.

3. *Let clothes soak according to the manufacturer's instructions and how dirty they are.* (She helpfully elaborates on this later too. Really dirty stuff – their farming clothes – she soaks for at least 24 hours. And, she says, if she's busy and doesn't get around to the washing for a couple of days she adds a capful of chlorine bleach to the wash water to stop it 'smelling like it died'. A minimum soak should be three hours, but delicates should be washed after 15–30 minutes of soaking. Oh – and don't use hot water, she says. It's a waste of resources and can damage your clothes.

4. *Agitate each article separately by rubbing between your hands about five times.*

5. *Squeeze out excess water and throw article into rinse tub.*

6. *Swish the clothes a few times to rinse them.*

7. *Squeeze excess water out of the clothing and place it in a bucket.*

8. *Carry the bucket of clothes out and hang them up to dry.*

Don't bother with washboards, she admonishes. (Can you even buy a washboard any more?) 'Too much work. Will also leave you open to "grandma" jokes from your spouse.' Nor is she a fan of wringers. 'Forget 'em. Wringers break buttons and zippers, take up your time and work you to death.' Her final piece of advice: 'insist on familial participation in this event...You will be richly rewarded with clean clothes, a clean environment, and a family that knows the joy of shared responsibilities.'

Ludo, I can tell, is not at all convinced by the idea of a washing-machine-free life. I'm going to try it and I'll report back (although I suspect I'll have to do it without familial participation). Using sunshine and fresh air instead of a dryer, I do get. We have a dryer, but

I only use it when there is no hope of anything getting dry outdoors. And I do take curious pleasure in pegging things on a line. There's something meditative about it.

We were back at our cabin in early spring. I'd been in London and had had a sobering sort of a day. First thing in the morning I was on Sky News. I'd been asked to talk about the scourge of plastic – which finally, after many years of campaigning by various charities, NGOs and concerned individuals, is being taken seriously. Suddenly plastic and the effect it has on our environment and on wildlife is headline news. The public is horrified, outraged, demanding businesses and government respond. 'Can I just ask you one more thing?' the presenter said before she wrapped up the interview. 'What do you think of the climate-change protests that are causing major disruption in London this week?'

This was the other big news. A group calling itself Extinction Rebellion had taken to the streets of London. Through peaceful protest and mass civil disruption, their aim was to get the issue of climate change on the global agenda. Like the problem of plastic, climate change has been a cause of deep concern for scientists and environmentalists for decades. It is not a new phenomenon. But governments and society have, until now, chosen to ignore it or deny that it is happening at all. My interviewer is not very good at hiding her frustration with the protests that for several days have blocked roads in central London and caused traffic to gridlock. I know she is hoping that I will agree with her unspoken view and I know I'm going to disappoint her.

'I think what they are doing is magnificent,' I say. 'This is the greatest challenge the human race has ever faced. A few days of inconvenience is going to feel very insignificant when the very planet we live on is unable to sustain us any longer. Climate change is real, we are all experiencing the effects of it. Fires, water shortages, coastal erosion, extreme weather and the damage that causes to homes and infrastructure. And do you know what makes me so sad and so ashamed?' I don't wait for her to answer because I know she is desperate to end the interview and move on to the next story. 'It is our generation that discovered the climate is changing and that the change is happening as a direct result of our behaviour. And yet we've done nothing to stop it. Nothing. That is our legacy. Unless we do something decisive and meaningful now.' She gives me a rather strained 'thank you' and turns back to the camera to introduce the weather.

From the studio I go to meet a group of volunteers who have joined the group Thames 21 for a river clean-up. The low tide was earlier this morning, so the hundred or so people I see at the water's edge have already filled a large number of black bin bags. From the towpath the muddy bank below looks litter-free. I wonder if there is anything left to do. 'Oh, there is plenty,' Paul tells me, handing me a garden fork. 'Just dig there.' I sink the fork into the mud and lever it up. Tangled amongst the tines of the fork is a fibrous mass. 'Wet wipes,' says Paul, matter-of-factly. 'Flush 'em down the loo and they end up here. The whole bank is basically a solid mass of 'em. We've found the odd plastic bottle, a few discarded cans, that sort of thing, but most of those bags at the top there are filled with wet wipes.' And over the next couple of hours we filled yet more bags from the seemingly endless supply before the incoming tide chased us off the mud.

I took a commuter train from Charing Cross and rattled through the suburbs to Kent. Ludo met me at the station with the dogs and we went to stay with friends for the night before taking the early train beneath the Channel and driving south. It's six or seven hours from Calais, but we listen to podcasts, stop when we see a good place to let the dogs out for a stretch, and find a village café for lunch. The last hour or so we're on country roads that wind through fields and woodland, past small farms and villages that are so quiet they appear abandoned. There are few other cars on the road, the sun is bright and warm, the countryside fresh, green, bursting with new life. It is the perfect spring day. All the worries and pressures that crowd in on normal, day-to-day life seem irrelevant and inconsequential here, and our brains relax and just enjoy taking in our surroundings.

It has become a ritual of mine to walk the last mile of the journey. Ludo pulls into the side of the road at the top of a path that disappears into the woods. The dogs and I jump out and wave him off before plunging into the dappled shade of the sweet chestnuts. I walk slowly, savouring every step, breathing in the fresh, sappy scent of new leaves. We reach the edge of the trees and walk through grass and wildflowers. Insects buzz, birds flit amongst the hedgerows. We come to the top of the stony track that leads down to our cabin. The dogs recognize it and start to run, although there is still about half a mile to go. But still I don't rush. I love this walk, love recalling the first time we came here with Bob and Di, bumping over the ruts and rocks, entering the cathedral-like gloom of a forest of conifers, descending towards a break in the trees. The track comes to an abrupt end at the edge of the wood. I remember getting out of the car, walking down a grass slope and exclaiming as the lake came into view. It was a fairy tale, a hidden glade and I loved it on sight. And that feeling has never diminished. It is still magical; Narnia without the need for a wardrobe.

In the morning I get up at dawn, let myself out into the chilly half-light, the eastern sky streaked with pink and orange, heralding the sun that is yet to appear. I've been under the weather recently, had a cold, a miserable debilitating bug: not bad enough to keep me in bed but bad enough that I wish it had. Two weeks of snot and phlegm, a hacking cough and a rasping voice. Today is the first day I've felt able to move at a pace faster than an achy walk and, with my dog loping effortlessly ahead, I break into a tentative run, relishing the freshness of the morning air, the feel of leaf litter and stone beneath my feet, the early beginnings of the dawn chorus that seems somehow to emphasize the deep silence of the still-sleeping countryside. We run, dog and I, up the track through the woods and fields full of bright spring grass and dandelion clocks. There are violets in the hedgerow, a small white flower I don't know the name of and the first bluebells. In the field at the top of the lane are cows and their tiny calves, perfect copper-coloured miniatures of their mothers, who give low warning moos as we pass, hustling their offspring away from the fence and into the centre of the field. We come into the little hamlet at the top of the track – barely a hamlet really, just a handful of houses and a farm – cross the grey ribbon of empty road to skirt along the edge of fields and over a stream. Uphill we go, towards the old church of the neighbouring village up on the skyline, the dark orange sphere of the sun just appearing above the trees behind it.

It is a week of simple pleasures. There are tasks to do, as there always are when we open up the cabin for the first time after the winter, small fixes to make, herbs to re-pot, brambles to cut back, but because we don't have to fit in doing them around an already busy working day, they don't feel onerous. A job that always needs doing – and we both love – is chopping and stacking wood. This part of France is full of trees – mainly chestnut and oak, although walnut is grown too – and in autumn there are stalls at the local market piled high with the nuts and bottles of their rich, fragrant oil. There are small timber mills everywhere – usually one-man affairs – and every household has a woodpile. There is something extraordinarily appealing and satisfying about a beautifully cut and stacked pile of wood. Lars Mytting's book *Norwegian Wood: Chopping, Stacking and Drying Wood the Scandinavian Way* garnered an almost evangelical following and became a bestseller. And you get the feeling Thoreau almost swoons at the sight of his woodpile:

> *Every man looks at his woodpile with some kind of affection. I love to have mine before my window, and the more chips the better to remind me of my pleasing work.*

And the woodpiles stacked at the edge of fields, outside barns and in gardens here inspire admiration and envy in equal measure. Perfectly equal lengths of wood are stacked in precise order, chest-high and many metres long. The top will be protected by a tarpaulin, roped tightly down, the sides left exposed to the air to season the logs. Needless to say, we cannot lay claim to a woodpile like that, but when we were here last summer Ludo built a long, roofed structure behind our cabin and we spent many happy hours with chainsaw and axe cutting the logs to fill it. Ludo has the eye and the patience for stacking, which is not unlike doing a jigsaw or building a dry-stone wall. I love the physicality of swinging an axe, the enormous satisfaction when a log splits cleanly from one, perfectly judged blow. It's good teamwork, pleasingly tiring and mucky too. When the pile is replenished, we jump, sweaty, grimy and covered in sawdust, into the cool, dark water of the lake. Oh, how I love that feeling! And then we sit, bare skin on the sun-warmed wood of the deck, watching the colour starting to leech from the day, the air cooling, the call of a cuckoo against a backdrop of silence. This is the true pleasure of being here: just sitting – the feel of the wood, the smell of the evening, the sounds of the end of the day. These are things that cost nothing, yet can be so hard to attain. These apparently inconsequential things are overlooked or overrun by our busy, overcrowded, noisy world, but they are not inconsequential. They make us feel alive. Present. And that has become something rare. A privilege. And it's now we understand that changing the cabin, adding rooms, trying to find ways to make it more – well, like a normal house – would destroy the very thing that makes it so special. It may be too basic, too simple, to be practical for everyday living, but it's that very simplicity that makes it a place of respite and retreat, appreciated all the more because it is different.

But is there a middle ground? Can the privilege of conscious stillness become part of the pattern of a day, rather than a rare moment to treasure? Is there a way of incorporating that essence of simplicity, and the deep contentment it brings, into our everyday lives?

FIRST STEPS: TAKING STOCK
*

I have a fear of clutter and mess. I'm not sure it counts as a phobia, but if it does, it's got a rather wonderful name: ataxophobia. The root of this fear is, I think, something to do with my need for order in just one area of my life. I feel that if at least I can have some semblance of control over the domestic bit of it, it mitigates the almost complete lack of influence I have over the working bit. In common with many self-employed freelancers, I can lurch between being so busy there's barely time to breathe and the stomach-churning anxiety of an empty diary. And I never know how a year is going to pan out; can't even guess what I might earn or whether I'll work for fifty weeks or five.

So in order not to feel like a helpless piece of jetsam tossed about by the choppy waves of life, home needs to be a refuge, a place of calm; which it is, but only if it is tidy and there aren't piles of extraneous stuff all over the place. That is not to say that I aspire to living with only the bare essentials. I don't aim for minimalism, to live in the way Japanese writer Fumio Sasaki describes in his book *Goodbye, Things: The New Japanese Minimalism.* He pares down his possessions to such an extent that he can pack up everything he owns in less than half an hour.

I understand the liberation that might come with this, the euphoric feeling of being so unburdened, but I don't want to live in a white box with no furniture and one hand towel. I love my books, the things I've collected on my travels, the pictures on the walls of our house. And I like colour. Although I can never imagine living in a city again, if I had to, I would want to live in a house in the brightly coloured terrace in Bristol that I've often admired. Or in the row on the waterfront at

Tobermory. Somehow those houses seem more homely, more inviting, infinitely more appealing than the serried, formal rows of uniformly pale houses in the adjoining streets.

Edi Rama, now prime minister of Albania, used colour to transform the country's capital city and, in so doing, the mindset of the people living there. Rama trained as an artist but was also very politically active. He had been an ardent supporter of democracy, and was one of the key figures to influence the fall of Communism in the early 90s. In 1998 he was made Minister of Culture, Youth and Sports and instantly became known for his colourful way of dressing as well as his rather unorthodox political style. It garnered him a lot of support, particularly amongst young people, and in 2000 he was elected mayor of Albania's capital, Tirana.

Tirana was a city typical of the post-Communist era. Grey, concrete Eastern-bloc architecture, metal grids over shop windows, no green spaces. Crime and corruption were rife, the streets occupied by gangs. One of the very first things Rama did when he became mayor was to send out a team of people armed with pots of bright orange paint. Rama used his artist's love of colour and flamboyance to transform the city. He didn't have the budget to demolish buildings so instead he painted them, turning the uniformly grey and dismal cityscape into a riot of colour. And the effect was extraordinary. In an interview with an American journalist, Rama told him, 'when we started painting, two things would happen. First, people that had the shops would start to get rid of the grids (the bars over the windows) because they felt safer. And the second effect was that they started paying taxes.' Colour brought Tirana back to life, thousands of trees were planted, green spaces restored. It became a tourist attraction and in 2004 the award committee of the inaugural World Mayor Prize gave it to Rama.

The people we bought our house in Wales from had also liked colour. There were bright pink doors, egg-yellow walls and turquoise skirting boards. Although we didn't want to be swayed by today's fashion that demands our homes be zen-like temples of calming neutrals, the colours we had inherited were positively shouty. So we painted all the walls the same, inoffensive off-white. Our furniture, paintings, rugs and books provide the colour. And it is my refuge: we've lived there for 12 years – longer than anywhere I've ever lived in my adult life.

But in that time, we have accumulated stuff. Lots of it. And given that neither of us take much joy in shopping and both believe our requirements to be fairly basic, this is something of a mystery. But it is there – filling cupboards and shelves and rooms. Every now and then, I have felt a compulsion to do something about it. That week after Christmas is a favourite time. Maybe it's the 'in with the new, out with the old' spirit of the coming year.

One year I woke up very early and, as the rest of the household slept, emptied every cupboard in the kitchen. At first the feeling was euphoric. The joyful discovery and turfing out of long-out-of-date spices; almost empty sauce bottles – the sticky remnants encrusted in the bottom; ancient bags of flour; mouldy jam. I got rid of chipped mugs and glasses, burnt frying pans. Matched up the jumble of Tupperware in a drawer with its lids. I made a pile of dishes, bowls and utensils we didn't use or need to take to the charity shop. Sharpened knives, cleaned out the cupboard under the sink and found that, amongst the clutter of cleaning cloths, dishwasher tablets, tea towels and soap, we had, hidden in dark, inaccessible corners, enough washing-up liquid to last a decade.

And that's when the rest of the house started to wake up – my husband Ludo, the friends we had staying, appearing in the kitchen, hoping for coffee. But the kitchen looked like a jumble sale. There was a pile of bin bags in the corner, every surface was covered in things, the table laden with all the jars and bottles and cans and packets of ingredients that weren't out of date or mouldy and that needed to be put back in some sort of order. And I suddenly felt weak with exhaustion. Gone was the initial excitement, the sense of achievement; instead I was overwhelmed by mess and disorder and thoroughly bored by the whole process.

It was a useful, if painful lesson; one that taught me not to try to do everything at once. And to take stock, make a plan, rather than just leap in and start hurling things out of cupboards. So that is what I'm doing now. Walking through the house, opening cupboards and drawers, making mental notes of those that need sorting out.

In Sweden this process goes by the name of *dostadning*. The literal translation is 'death cleaning', although according to Margaret Magnusson (who describes herself as somewhere between 80 and 100 years old) you don't have to be in your final years to indulge in a bit of *dostadning*. 'Death cleaning is not about dusting or mopping up,' she writes in her surprisingly uplifting book, *The Gentle Art of Swedish Death Cleaning*, 'it is about a permanent form of organization that makes your everyday life run more smoothly...The intention is not that we should remove things that make our lives pleasant and more comfortable. But if you can't keep track of your things, then you know you have too much.'

We all have different ways of taking stock, of deciding what we want in our lives – the things that give us real pleasure – and the accumulated, extraneous things that don't. 'Keep what sparks joy,' Japanese tidying guru Marie Kondo tells us. 'Tidy your space, transform your life.' Have you watched her show, by the way? It's oddly compelling for a programme that devotes quite a lot of time to how to organize your Tupperware and the most efficient way to fold your knickers. And when you see what other people have crammed in their cupboards, attics and garages, it can make your own over-stuffed home feel positively spartan in comparison.

I can't imagine my house without books, and although we have a lot of them, they sit, carefully ordered, on floor-to-ceiling shelves that line the sitting room on three sides. I love being in that room, surrounded by the colourful spines of hundreds of books. And it is a particular pleasure, because before these shelves were built, we had books all over the house, on window-ledges, propped up on the top of bits of furniture or just in piles. If we wanted to find a particular book it could take hours. Now they are no longer clutter, they do indeed spark joy, and that, for me, is the key.

Jennifer – the woman I hoped might help me overcome my total inability to make bread (of which, more later) – is the one who told me about 'death cleaning'. 'Clearing a house of the things that belonged to someone you loved after they have died is soul destroying,' she said, with a depth of feeling that comes from experience. I know. Even packing up the few of my dad's things from his room in the nursing home the morning he died required me to mentally shut down the emotional side of my brain and go at the task almost blindly, like an automaton.

And Mum has been courageously – and it really does take courage – going through the house in the months that have followed, tackling cupboards and drawers. Recently she emailed me a photograph of a kitchen drawer with the triumphant caption 'LOOK!!!!' I had been staying a few weeks before and was cooking us supper. In the course of trying to track down a vegetable peeler I had opened a drawer rammed with utensils, some of which I swear I remember Mum having when I was a child. And there is nothing wrong with that, if they work. But these were wonky tin-openers, blunt peelers, rusting spoons, all crowded in with the new ones she had bought to replace them. And the kitchen knives were shoved in amongst them all too.

'That's why they are all blunt,' I told her. 'Honestly, Mum, I don't know how you find anything in here at all.'

She gave me a look which said, quite plainly (and justifiably), 'piss off – it's my kitchen' – but something must have resonated, because the photo she sent was of a beautifully ordered drawer containing just the few utensils she needs and the knives carefully stowed in a knife block.

'Wow! You're amazing!' I write back. 'Now just the twenty-eight drawers of wrapping paper to go through...'

Jennifer, who is my age, says she's already started death cleaning.

'I've been on a mission, getting rid of stuff and going back to basics. It does scare me a bit, because so much of what we have is part of us, part of our lives, but it is also very liberating.'

I'm guessing, but I suspect that clothes take up more space in our lives than any of our other possessions. I don't buy clothes very often (it is one of my least favourite ways of spending time, equal, perhaps, to having a manicure), but when I do I'll often buy quite a few things at once with the view that I won't need to go clothes shopping again for ages. But inevitably I end up with things I wear only a handful of times and there are items I find during my periodic bouts of sorting that still have their labels on. And the remorse I feel is painful.

Camille (who, again, you will meet properly later) came up with an excellent way to counter her over-buying habit. Not that she believed she had one.

'I thought I was a good egg!' she told me in her soft French accent. 'I thought I don't buy very much, but I just wanted to check.' So she made a list of all the things she had bought the previous year and was shocked. 'It turned out I did buy loads of things – clothes, shoes, all sorts.' She then listed the things she had made – she is a seamstress – and discovered that she had been more productive than she realized. In light of knowing exactly what she had, she wrote another list of what she needed for the year ahead. 'And it turned out not to be much – new socks, new underwear, a pair of shoes, and then there were a few other things which I could make, or mend or adjust from clothes I already had.'

It was, she said, a really worthwhile exercise that helped bring into focus exactly what she had and what she needed, killing the 'I want, therefore I'll buy' impulse we all get swept along by occasionally.

I did a clothes sort at the onset of winter, going through the summery clothes I was putting away in the spare room wardrobe, and re-evaluating what I had to get me through the colder months ahead. I tried on a few things to see whether I still liked them, or that they fitted, and made a pile of the things I didn't want to keep or knew I wouldn't wear. There were some decent pairs of shoes, too – smart ones that have rarely seen the light of day – and a couple of winter coats. I would usually take them to the local charity shops, but this time, inspired by my dad, I contacted my local women's refuge to see if they might be useful there.

In the 70s my dad worked in an office in West London. It was opposite a building that was the headquarters of an organization called Chiswick Women's Aid – the world's first refuge for women and children escaping domestic violence. Over the years it became a registered charity and changed its name to Refuge. Today, it provides a national network of safehouses and services for those forced to flee their homes. My dad had been a staunch supporter of the charity since its earliest days – something I only discovered just before he died. The women the charity supports often arrive with few possessions and little money. Donations of good-quality clothes, clothes they can wear to go to job interviews or to work, can be a real help.

The cupboard I discover that is in urgent need of attention is just outside the bathroom. It is one we created when we moved in, by boxing in a slightly odd-shaped space left around some pipework. And it has proved fantastically useful for storing things like bottles of sun cream, packets of soap, spare loo paper and basic medical supplies. It's quite big – bigger than most bathroom cupboards – but in the same way that Parkinson's law states that 'work expands so as to fill the time available for its completion', stuff has a habit of accumulating to fill any available space. And this cupboard is the physical embodiment of that phenomenon.

Ludo has a habit of buying things in a way I describe as 'siege-mentality shopping'. On occasion he will come home with enough loo paper, or boxes of matches, or packets of biscuits to see us right for a year. Light bulbs are the other things he seems to have a deep-rooted fear of running out of. There is an entire cupboard downstairs that is overflowing with light bulbs of various sorts – so many they are now piled up on the top of the cupboard too, and some are so old they were banned by the EU half a decade ago. And plasters. On the shelf in front of me are boxes and boxes of plasters, all of them open, squashed and spilling their contents amongst the multiple packets of aspirin, cold remedies, anti-inflammatories, tubes of antiseptics and bottles of cough mixture. I square my shoulders. I will start here.

Simple Pleasure #1
— ORDER RESTORED —

I begin with the top shelf because it is the least daunting. There are three shelves altogether and then a jumble of bags full of who-knows-what and a sewing machine stowed underneath them. The sewing machine is not mine. This is another thing I have a deep-rooted fear of – not the actual machine, just using it. It dates back to my school days and I have plans to address it, just not quite yet. Ludo bought the sewing machine with the admirable intention of using it to mend various items of clothing: jeans that needed patching – that sort of thing. I had no idea he could use a sewing machine and was rather impressed and not a little envious. In a flurry of enthusiasm, it was set up on the kitchen table and before long Ludo was parading his newly mended jeans with justifiable pride. The sewing machine has been in the bottom of the cupboard ever since.

The top shelf has a comprehensive array of sun creams from factor 50 down to what appears to be just neat oil. There are after-sun lotions and multiple tubes, cans and sprays of insect repellent, my favourite being one I remember buying in the Swedish Arctic, where mosquitos are the size of small birds and clothes prove no deterrent. It is called 'OFF!' Works like a charm.

I take the whole lot off the shelf and sit on the floor to sort them, discarding all the almost-empty bottles, any sun cream with a factor of less than 15, anything with DEET in it, because my skin doesn't like it (which is annoying, because mosquitos love me) and anything out of date. I wipe perhaps a decade's worth of dust off the shelf and restock it in the manner of a pharmacy, marvelling at (and mildly horrified by) my ability to be so damn anal. And when I'm done, I actually step back to admire my handiwork with a happy surge of achievement. 'I will be back,' I say to the cupboard in my best Schwarzenegger voice, then I close the door and go and have a celebratory cup of tea.

I can't face tackling the middle shelf – the one with the plasters and pills. I will need to be in a particular frame of mind to take that one on. But a couple of days later I clear out the third shelf (travel adaptors, spongebags, lots of little bottles of shampoo and bars of soap filched from hotel rooms) and the space beneath it, unearthing bags of old, torn sheets, shirts with holes in the armpits, more jeans with worn out knees – all, presumably, awaiting repair, but long since forgotten and replaced.

I return to finish the job in the middle of the night. Insomnia, the curse of so many of us middle-aged women, can have its advantages. No one is entirely sane at three o'clock in the morning, and a level of insanity is exactly what is required to take on that lurking chaos. Ludo is away, working abroad. I can do this without him ever knowing how deranged I am.

It takes a very long time. The date stamps on medicine bottles and pill packets are often hard to find and then so small and faded they are almost impossible to decipher. Reading glasses might have helped, and I have a pair – somewhere – but instead I just hold the packets very close to my face in the glare of the light above the mirror in the bathroom. By the time the sky is streaked with the pale light of the coming dawn, our stock of medicines is reduced by two-thirds and is arranged by category (colds, headaches, upset stomachs), the nine separate packets of plasters (yes, nine) are now combined and contained in one empty ice-cream tub (without its lid, so they are easy to get at if either of us is dripping blood all over the place), and beside me is a satisfyingly weighty black bin bag. My work is done. I shower, dress and go out to feed the animals feeling light-hearted and unburdened. By lunchtime, of course, I'm fractious with exhaustion, but it doesn't matter, because all I need to do is go upstairs and look inside that cupboard to be instantly restored.

*

THE SIMPLICITY GURU
*

Ideas that feel absolutely right one day can seem less right, or even ridiculous, on another. I have occasionally found myself wondering whether this hankering to shift life's focus, to pare it down and declutter it, isn't some sort of mid-life crisis, a phase that will pass. But according to Satish Kumar, my timing is pretty typical. Satish co-founded the Schumacher College in Devon. The courses it offers are in ecology and horticulture, with the emphasis on working in partnership with nature. Many of the people who come to the college to study are between 40 and 50. They've got houses, jobs, money, cars – the trappings of working life in the Western world – but they have come to the realization that they are not content, that their material possessions don't count for anything very much and the jobs they are doing bring in money, but little in the way of personal satisfaction. And that although they may be employable, they don't have any of the practical skills that give a true feeling of purpose and worth. They don't know how to grow food, build a house, or use their creativity or imaginations to do something useful in the world. They are dependent on other people to do these things on their behalf. But they do know that if they just had time, they would not only be able to learn these skills, but also garner immense pleasure and satisfaction from doing so.

Tim Dickens is a bit younger than the average student – in his early thirties. When his life went awry, as lives have a habit of doing, he felt an irrepressible draw to the land and sought solace in its earthy rootedness. Which would make perfect sense if Tim had grown up on a farm or even somewhere rural, but he hadn't. His childhood was spent in suburban Essex, on the edge of the Thames estuary. He joined the sea scouts and would go sailing at the weekends. His father was a GP, his mum a practice nurse, and Tim, his brother and sister went to the local grammar school. It was, he said, pushing his hair out of his eyes and squinting in the evening sun, a very normal, middle-class upbringing. As normal as it can be.

Although both his parents were medics, there was no pressure for their children to follow suit. But they were expected to strive academically – aim for Oxbridge – and Tim admits to being rather lazy, 'which got me in trouble'. He dropped out of grammar school, taking his A-levels at a local college, and scraped a place at Exeter University to read languages. 'Then there is this expectation that you will do the graduate-recruitment thing. People come from accountancy firms and stockbrokers, various banks. They take you out for beers and talk about what it is like to work for them, encourage you to join their graduate schemes. And that was what all my friends were doing, but I just felt uncomfortable with the whole idea. I had no interest in maths or economics and couldn't quite see how I would fit in.'

It was journalism that Tim wanted to pursue. 'I had the notion of becoming a newspaper journalist and ending up as editor of the *Guardian* by a certain age – 30 or something!' So he followed his friends to London, but instead of going to work in the City, he started working for local newspapers in the suburbs. The year was 2008, a time of economic upheaval and also a time when print media was struggling to compete with the appeal and the potential of the internet. He was made redundant twice, but he also became increasingly disillusioned with the industry. He looks pained as he recalls being sent to knock on the door of the house of someone who had just lost their son in a horrible stabbing incident and ask them if he could write a tribute. 'And I went, but I felt terrible doing it. They slammed the door in my face. I phoned my editor and he just said, "Go back and knock on the door again." It made me feel grimy and deeply uncomfortable that this was the sort of thing the media believed we all wanted to read about.' He also started to realize that he was not going to be made editor of the *Guardian* any time soon.

So he made the decision to leave his job, despite having no savings, and, with a friend, set up a community newspaper in Brixton, south London, where he was living. He did it, he said, to try and redress the balance, give coverage to local things – both good and bad – that were being ignored by other papers. Do it ethically, involve the community. He ran the paper for three years, first as a website and then in print. At first he had to do other things – 'kid's parties was one of them' – to earn money, but eventually the paper was able to pay its way and provide him with a small salary, just enough to live on. It was also gaining a reputation. Tim and his friend were nominated for awards, invited to conferences to discuss how best to engage and bring together communities, interviewed on BBC News. 'But we had to work really, really, really hard. We'd work through the night, two or three nights in a row and every weekend and I got more and more knackered. I was heading towards burnout.'

It was the exhaustion that Tim thinks made him start to lose interest in the project, even though it was being feted, and his friends and, importantly for him, his parents recognized its success. He also wanted to earn a bit more money and he knew the paper (which is still running today) would be unlikely ever to be able to give him a pay rise.

So he accepted a job as a head of digital communications. It was well-paid, easy 9–5 work, four days a week – a stark contrast to his working life at the paper – with plenty of opportunities to mix with the glitz and glamour of London's media world. It seemed the perfect next step. But it wasn't. Not only did he not enjoy the work or being in a sterile office, he found himself becoming increasingly stressed and anxious. On the way to an important meeting, he had a panic attack in a lift and had to confess to his boss who was with him that he just couldn't function. And this would start to happen more and more frequently.

He sought respite in the overgrown garden of his ex-council flat in south London.

'I called it Florence Farm! I had this idea in my head to make it as productive as possible. I don't know how I knew what to do – I didn't really – I asked my dad, who's a keen gardener, and read John Seymour's guide to self-sufficiency. I made the lawn into vegetable beds, brought in manure from the riding stables in Dulwich. I did so much digging and I just loved every minute of it. I remember one time I had to come home in the middle of the day because I felt overwhelmed with anxiety and I went straight out into the garden. It was summer and I stayed out there until it got dark and by the end of the day I felt so much better. I think there is something therapeutic about having your hands in the soil, being in touch with it and doing something physical that has an outcome: grow a courgette or a tomato and you can eat it. And it was at this time that I realized that being in a garden, doing stuff with my hands, was what I wanted to do. When I left the paper, I thought having a bigger salary would make my life better. It's a human trait, I think, to always want more than you've got, but the joy I discovered from growing vegetables was infinitely greater than any happiness I got from earning a big salary.'

Tim left London and went, first of all, to work as a volunteer at a charity called Jamie's Farm, which is actually based at five different farms in the south and west of the country. It supports young people, vulnerable people at risk from social and academic exclusion, through farming and therapy. Now he is four months into a six-month residential horticultural course at Schumacher. The evening light is mellowing. He shows me around the five-acre plot the students cultivate. I admire the abundance and variety of things they grow, all of which are used in the college kitchens. Together, we shut the chickens in their fox-proof run for the night. I wonder what he might do when the course is finished. He is still pondering that, he says; doesn't yet have a fixed plan of where this phase of his life will lead him. He likes the idea of eventually having some land and creating somewhere for people going through similar experiences to his own to visit, a place where they can witness, experience and learn a different way of living and working.

'When did you last have a panic attack?' I ask.

'A long time ago. Not since I left London.' He pauses. Smiles. 'I'm so much happier. This morning I got up at 6.30 and walked down to swim in the river as the sun came up over the trees. I came back through the woods, listening to the hum of the bees and insects. In London my day would start later, listening to the *Today* programme, rushing, fighting to get on the tube or cycling through the traffic. An old friend from London came to see me a couple of weeks ago. We were really close – I was at his wedding. And all he talked about was the new, bigger house he's bought and how he's traded his car in for the latest BMW. It all felt so alien and I don't think he understood at all why I find this way of life so enriching, even though I'm earning nothing. It's hard to explain to him and many of my old friends why what I'm doing is so important to me, but I have no doubts at all that this is right.'

Tim's desire to do something more physical, more tangible, more useful is common amongst many of the people who enrol at the college. And it is a feeling that is increasingly familiar to me, too. But where, I ask Satish, does this desire that is apparently so prevalent come from?

Satish smiles his big, generous smile.

'It's innate. It's intrinsic to human nature. Our hands are made to make. But our society and the way we educate our children dismisses manual labour – it is only for those who have failed, who are not intellectually up to doing anything else. And because of this attitude, instead of being a society of makers we are a society of consumers, dependent on buying everything we need and easily swayed into buying so much we don't.'

Satish is not alone in thinking this way. An essay in *The Plain Reader* tells how the children growing up in the Amish and Mennonite Community of Cookeville, Tennessee, go to school at 7.30 in the morning and come home at 12.30. They have lunch with their families and then spend the afternoon learning how to do something useful with their hands. The author comments: 'head knowledge has its place, but most people in North America would be better off with a few more callouses on their hands'.

Satish is a well-known advocate of simple living and has written widely on the subject. I'd heard of him because my neighbour, the eminent ecologist Herbert Girardet, worked with Satish at *Resurgence* magazine and they continue to collaborate on various projects. I had bumped into Herbie and his wife Barbara a week or so earlier while walking our dogs. When they asked what I was up to, I told them I was exploring this idea of simplicity that had crept up on me, knowing – well, hoping – that rather than thinking I had gone slightly mad, they would understand.

'It seems', I said, as we stood in the dappled evening shade of the beech trees, the dogs milling around our legs, 'that contentment and simplicity are intrinsic. That the reason so many of us in Western society are not content is that we live lives that are over-crowded and over-complicated. We've confused simplicity with convenience. But convenience doesn't seem to bring happiness.'

And then I stood, looking at my feet, feeling a little bit embarrassed.

Herbie and Barbara looked at each other and then back at me and said, in unison, 'You should go and see Satish...'

And so, after a day working down in Exeter, instead of driving home I went on, further into Devon, to meet the man who has spent a lifetime living simply. I arrived as supper was being laid out for the residential students and staff – bowls of salad and vegetables all grown in the gardens by Tim and the others on his course. Alongside were big crusty loaves of home-made bread, fruit and cheese. I was invited to help myself to a plateful and join Satish, who was already seated at a table outside in the evening sun. My first thought on seeing him was: 'This man can't possibly be 83 years old.' Immaculately dressed in khakis and a crisp, pale blue shirt, with a phone and pen in the pocket, he was spry and dapper, and radiated such extraordinary energy it was like being caught up in a magnetic field. His smile is huge and lights up his eyes and his whole face, and he almost bounces when he talks.

He was born in India in 1936 and, when he was just nine years old, he became a Jain monk. Two of the principles of Jainism are non-violence and asceticism, so as a monk, Satish had a strictly vegetarian diet and had to renounce all property and social relations, own nothing and be attached to no one.

He lived this life for 11 years, itinerant and relying on being given food by strangers, and perhaps would have continued to do so had he not read a book by Mahatma Gandhi. So inspired was he, he ran away to become a student of one of Gandhi's most eminent disciples, and in 1962, along with a friend, decided to undertake a peace walk to protest against the atomic bomb. They travelled on foot, with no money, from India to the four capitals of the nuclear world: Moscow, Paris, London and Washington DC, staying with anyone along the way who would offer them food or shelter.

As a prominent peace activist, he returned to the UK in the early 70s for a conference. It was there that he met E F Schumacher, an economist, whose book *Small is Beautiful: A Study of Economics as if People Mattered* was ranked by the *Times Literary Supplement* in the top 100 most influential books published since the Second World War. Schumacher persuaded Satish not to go back to India, but to stay in the UK.

'There are many Gandhians in India,' he said to Satish. 'We need one here in England, to teach us these ideas of peace, simplicity, ecology, how to care for our environment, the importance of arts and crafts, creativity and imagination.'

And so Satish stayed, and when Schumacher died just a few years later, Satish continued the mission they had started together and he shows no signs of slowing down. He lectures, he writes books, he fundraises for the college. And although he is no longer living the life of a penniless monk or wandering peace activist, it is a simple life.

'But what is that?' I ask. 'Is a simple life one without any sort of comfort? Do you have to live in a cave and hope that some kind person will bring you the occasional bowl of gruel?'

Satish laughs.

'No, no, no, no, no!' he admonishes, his eyes sparkling. 'Simplicity is not hair-shirt living. It can be comfortable, you can still have beautiful things, but the key is not to be wasteful. Waste is the curse of our civilization. Because that waste – the endless stuff we buy and then throw away – is polluting our air, our soil, our water, the very things we need to survive. We can have beautiful things, but they should also be useful and durable, things that last and that you treasure. We can all have a good life if we live in a society that is less wasteful and less polluting.'

Are we willing to live differently, I wonder? Have we become too entrenched in our consumer ways? Satish is of the view that we may not have a choice, because the way we live is simply not sustainable in the long term. 'If we didn't think we needed so much, we wouldn't need to produce things in such volume. And we wouldn't need to work so much because we wouldn't need as much money. We'd have time to do things we want to do, things that are meaningful and joyful.'

We say goodbye, a handshake that turns into a hug.

'What's your secret?' I say. He looks at me quizzically. 'Your energy, your optimism...?'

'I garden. I cook. I walk.'

Getting Down and Dirty

GROWING PAINS PART 1
*

Emma and I realized we were kindred spirits the moment we met. As I went to shake her hand I noted that her jeans, like mine, were covered in muddy paw prints.

'Oh my God!' she exclaimed, before she'd even said hello. 'You wear Crocs too!' and we both looked down at our feet, identically shod in the world's ugliest but most useful shoes.

Within minutes we had discovered that we had been born one day apart (she's older by a day, which I never tire of reminding her) and we share a loathing of marigolds, but had developed in recent months an obsession with dahlias. This is obviously something that just happens when you turn 50. 'Not that I've ever grown them,' I confessed. 'But there is something so fabulously flouncy about them. And don't they just keep flowering for months?'

Emma nodded.

'They're brilliant. So you want dahlias. What else?'

'Come and have a look,' I said.

The 4 acres of land that come with our house are mainly pasture. There's the field where we built a pond and planted fruit trees and sweet chestnuts, where the chickens and ducks live. There are two small, adjoining fields where the pigs live and then four paddocks and a big field that slopes steeply down to the woods for the sheep. The area on the south side of the house – which is probably about half an acre – is garden. I grew up with a garden. It was a lovely, rambling space with trees to climb and endless places to build camps, and I even had my own little vegetable patch where I grew radishes and carrots and runner beans.

My maternal grandfather, Stanley, was a great gardener. One of my earliest memories is of going to visit him and my grandmother in the tiny cottage they rented on a large country estate. The cottage had a small garden full of flowers, but Stan had also been given permission to grow vegetables in the estate's greenhouses. I remember so well going into them with him, of being hit by the damp, fuggy warmth, the smell of soil and greenery as we stepped through the door. He would urge me to pick the pods off the pea plants, hard-packed and slightly knobbly from the peas lying tight inside, waiting to be released. I never liked peas as a young child. They were in the same category as things like baked beans and kidney beans (both of which I still can't abide). It's something about the texture, more than anything, I think. But Stan converted me to peas, showing me how to prise the pods open and run a finger down the neatly ordered line of little green spheres to release them, popping them into our mouths, relishing their sweet, green crunch.

We would walk on between the fragrant rows of his tomato plants, rubbing the leaves in our fingers and delighting in their scent. But it was the tomatoes themselves that were so unforgettable. Reaching for and plucking the red, sun-warmed fruits and eating them whole; the soft crunch of the flesh and the slippery coolness of the seeds; the explosion of sweet–sour flavour. In my food top ten, tomatoes would be right up there.

My grandfather's tomato-growing prowess has not been passed down to me. Not that I really had had anywhere to practise after I left home, as every place where I had lived until now had either no garden or a very small urban patch of paving and pots. We did have an allotment for a couple of years when we lived in London and I loved it. London's benevolent climate, together with steaming sacks of horse manure from Ealing riding stables, made it fantastically productive and we would often grow more vegetables than we knew what to do with. I remember one year growing butternut squash for the first time and being absolutely delighted when we were able to harvest the first one. But they kept on coming and soon we were overrun. We gave them away, taking them to friends when we were invited for dinner (they would much rather have had wine), offering them to other people on neighbouring allotments.

So when we moved to the countryside one of the first things we did in our new, slightly daunting garden was to create an area to grow vegetables. And there was the perfect place: south facing and protected from north winds by an outbuilding. It wasn't too big. We knew from our allotment experience that we didn't need an enormous amount of space to grow plenty of vegetables for the two of us, and also how much work it is to tend it.

The only problem was that this perfect spot was completely choked up with nettles and brambles. But it was early in the year. The nettles and brambles were still young and small and we had recently taken possession of two pigs. Duffy and Delilah proved to be quite brilliant rotavators and had the patch cleared in a couple of weeks. We built four raised beds and put up a small polytunnel for the wonderful tomatoes that I was going to grow in honour of my grandfather.

It transpires that it is a lot harder growing vegetables almost 300 metres up a Welsh hillside than it is on a London allotment. And our raised beds weren't raised enough to deter our lovely but insatiable wildlife. Nor did the polytunnel give me a bounty of beautiful, flavoursome tomatoes, although I'm not sure the polytunnel can really take all the blame. And whilst we'd been dedicating our time to the vegetable garden, in the belief that the rest of the garden was what gardeners call 'well-established' and therefore, we thought, could look after itself, it had become a rampant jungle. In despair we found someone who could help keep some semblance of order, but in truth we'd lost confidence, lost heart and eventually, rather shamefully, lost interest.

Then, a couple of years ago it struck me how ludicrous it was that we had this beautiful outdoor space and spent so little time in it. It didn't even feel like ours. So I determined that we would go back to looking after it ourselves. We made a valiant effort. We weeded and strimmed, cut back and cleared. We redesigned the vegetable garden, making the raised beds smaller and more raised, and replacing the polytunnel with a proper greenhouse.

'Is it a sign of true middle age if you feel ludicrously happy to own a greenhouse?' I asked Ludo.

'Yes,' he said, without pause, and went back to (slightly grumpily) pushing the mower up and down.

But that nagging sense of inadequacy, of simply not knowing what to plant where, remained. We knew what we wanted to achieve but had no idea how to do it. It was Ludo who found Emma. Talked to her on the phone.

'I think you'll like her,' he told me. 'She doesn't like fuchsias either.'

*

As Emma and I walk around the garden together, I start to look at it afresh, as if through her eyes, and the stark realization hits me: the work Ludo and I have put in has not been nearly enough. Most of the beds are hopelessly overgrown. Any space between the wild tangle of shrubs and trees is choked with weeds and the plants unable to grow taller than a metre or more have just been swamped. I don't want a neat, prissy garden – 'You definitely haven't got one of those,' Emma laughs, perhaps to hide the sheer panic she is justified in feeling – but I do see now that our garden has gone beyond looking 'natural and wild' to being completely out of hand – more abandoned allotment than garden.

'Not keen on weeding?' Emma asks, with the merest hint of irony. It doesn't go unnoticed.

'Actually, I do quite like weeding,' I say, a tiny bit defensively, 'but I'm not very good at knowing what is weed and what isn't. And also they come back so bloody quickly. I've spent entire afternoons bent double in a flower bed pulling up weeds and two days later they're back with a vengeance.'

'Welcome to my world,' she says, dryly, in return.

We start to formulate a plan, one based around the amount of time I can actually spend working in the garden (realistically, probably not that much) and what I want the garden to do.

'My perfect garden would provide flowers for the house, vegetables and herbs for the kitchen and be wildlife friendly – plants that are good for butterflies, bees and other pollinators, hedges and trees that provide nest sites and food for birds – that sort of thing,' I say.

'So what we are aiming for,' says Emma, 'is low maintenance but beautiful and productive.'

'Like us,' I say.

And we cackle with laughter, standing on the lawn in our nasty plastic shoes, dirty jeans, even dirtier fingernails and no make-up.

*

For the plan to become action, a list is needed. The other thing we discover we have in common is we both love a list and the disproportionate satisfaction that comes from ticking something off it, however small. We sit at the kitchen table with mugs of coffee, a pile of seed catalogues and our notebooks. My notebook is new. I open its slim, unbleached cardboard cover printed with a design of red octopuses with wildly curling tentacles and it makes me think of my friend Jake.

Simple Pleasure #2

— AN UNEXPECTED PARCEL IN THE POST —

One of the great losses that has come with the invention of email is the joy of receiving a handwritten letter. We might still get the occasional one – a thank-you note or a postcard (although I don't think I can remember the last time I was sent one of those) – but generally our poor postmen and women, once so eagerly anticipated, now get to deliver little more than bills, catalogues and junk mail. But a week ago our postman bumped up our track in his van, as he does every day, his arrival heralded by cacophonous barking from the dogs, who are still excited to see him. I go out to meet him as he's swinging his big boots, at the end of bare legs, out of the door of his van. He is tall, skinny and tattooed and wears shorts every day of the year. 'Hiya,' we say in unison. 'There you go,' he says, handing me a bundle of what looks like the usual utility bills and rubbish. 'See you later,' and he roars off back down the hill.

I stand in the kitchen, sticking most of what he has handed me straight into the recycling bin, but then I come across an A5 brown envelope, my name and address handwritten in blue ink, Canadian stamps in the top right-hand corner. The envelope contains something more substantial than a letter – it is the size and weight of a slim book, which is what I guess must be in it. I ease my fingers beneath the glued-down flap and tip out the contents. Not one book, but four little notebooks with lined pages and each with a different design on the cover. There are the red octopuses. Another has a design of blue sharks; the third, lines of fish swimming in opposite directions; and the final one has a blue cover with a pattern of white anchors. There is no note, but I don't need one. There is only one person who would think to send me a parcel such as this.

Jake and I met when I was still living in London. We were amongst a dozen or so people sitting around a table having supper in a friend's garden. Ludo and I were both there, seated at opposite ends of the table next to people we didn't know, which can either make for a fun and interesting evening, or, if you find you have nothing in common at all, be excruciatingly dull. I was next to Jake, who is so far from being dull, I ignored, rather rudely, the person sitting on my other side.

Jake works for a global humanitarian organization and was then spending much of his life living alongside people who had survived, but been displaced by, war or a catastrophic natural disaster. It was Jake's job to co-ordinate all the logistics – food, water, shelter, sanitation, medical care – that are crucial to the lives of desperate, traumatized people who have often lost everything. It is harrowing work; dangerous too. He doesn't talk much about what he has witnessed in the last few months, but he has been living in Iraq, during and post the second Iraq war. His demeanour is cheerful, but his eyes look haunted. He has a break of a few weeks, he tells me, and then he will go somewhere else, probably Somalia.

'I'm going to the Swedish Arctic to research an article in a few days. I'm staying with a Sami family right out in the wilderness. You should come!' I say.

And I mean it, but I don't imagine for a moment he will.

But then, I didn't know Jake, didn't know his enviable ability to act on a whim, to be fearlessly, gloriously impetuous. At the end of the night, we swap telephone numbers and hug goodbye. 'See you soon, Kate', and the way he says it makes me think he will.

The following afternoon my phone rings. 'It's Jake. I've just booked my flight to Sweden. What do I need to bring? Shall we meet at the airport?'

We spend a week staying in a small, turf-covered hut on the edge of a lake and surrounded by the mountains and meadows of the Badjelannda National Park. It took a long day to hike here, carrying everything we would need. There are no roads and, apart from the small Sami camp where we are staying, no signs of human habitation. We walk for miles every day, take short, shrieking plunges into the lake, eat dark bread, dried reindeer meat and trout caught by our hosts and cooked on a fire. In the evenings, wrapped up against the chill, we sit, gloved hands around tin mugs of coffee, watching the glowing embers die down and trying to stay awake long enough to see the stars come out. We never manage – this far north in mid-August it is still light long after 10pm – and, by then, the Arctic air has overwhelmed us with contented exhaustion.

One night, towards the end of the week, I am jolted awake with a start by Jake's urgent command: 'Wake up!'

He is standing silhouetted in the doorway, his bare feet poking through the unzipped bottom of his sleeping bag.

'What time is it?' I ask, blearily.

'I don't know – one or something, but get up quick, you have to see this.'

I stagger and hop across the room in my sleeping bag, like a child in a sack race, to the open door. Jake grabs my hand and almost drags me outside.

'Look!' and he points to the sky, where ghostly streamers of silver-green light dance against its inky blackness. 'I've never seen the Northern Lights before,' breathes Jake, enraptured.

'Nor have I.'

And we stand in reverent silence and stare until they melt away into the dark and disappear.

Jake and I have been friends now for almost two decades. He lives and works in New York and sometimes we don't see each other, or speak, or have any contact at all for a year or more. And it makes no difference. It simply doesn't seem to matter. We just pick up where we left off. But if, out of the blue, the postman brings a handwritten letter or a parcel with no note, I know it will be from Jake. And the pleasure they give is immeasurable.

*

The list Emma and I are making is getting longer and longer. We start with vegetables.

'I don't think there is any point in growing something I can easily buy at the farm shop or the supermarket,' I say decisively, 'so I'd like to concentrate on either interesting varieties – heritage carrots in that lovely mix of colours, stripy beetroot, purple French beans – and then things that I wouldn't be able to buy locally.

'Like what?'

And I launch into a story about being taken out to lunch at an Ottolenghi restaurant and sharing a starter of what was no more than a few raw vegetables cut up into convenient chunks and a bowl of goo to dip them in. But, true to the reputation of the man, the goo was so delicious we were tempted to pick the bowl up and just lick it, and the vegetables that went with it, uncooked and unadorned, were spectacular, particularly one of them, which we couldn't identify. 'It's a watermelon radish,' said the waitress, when I asked. 'I'll get you one from the kitchen to show you.' And she returned with a rather unremarkable-looking root that resembled a turnip. Cut into it, though, and it has a watermelon-pink hue that gives it its name, a clean, crunchy texture and a beautiful flavour.

'So you want to grow those?' asks Emma, patiently.

'Yes, and I found a website where you can get the seeds, and seeds for loads of other interesting-looking things. I think we should try cucamelons, don't you?' Pushing the computer in front of her. 'And what about lemon cucumbers? And there are some really unusual chilli varieties here. And peppers. And aubergines. And how about these for spectacular tomatoes!' And I show her a picture of a tomato plant with deep purple-black fruits. They all go on the list as well as dwarf broad beans, peas, sorrel, sprouting broccoli, salad leaves, several other tomato varieties (I was already envisioning beautiful tomato salads thrown together in a casually artistic mix of colours, sizes and shapes) and three different types of strawberry.

'And finally,' I say, 'globe artichokes.'

'The plants are enormous,' points out Emma. 'We can't put them in the raised beds, they'll be no room for anything else.'

'I've got an idea where they can go,' I say confidently, 'but we've got to have them.'

Simple Pleasure #3

— THE RITUAL OF EATING A GLOBE ARTICHOKE —

I was wooed with a globe artichoke and it worked. Because the man doing the wooing has been my husband for the last 28 years. We hadn't been going out for very long. In fact, it may have been the first time I was invited to his house. I was slightly incredulous that our relationship had continued beyond our first date, which didn't end well. Although we had met several times before, I was terribly nervous, partly because I fancied him like mad and hoped he would feel the same, and partly because he was older, and therefore far more grown-up and sophisticated than me, and was taking me to a restaurant. I'd never done the 'dinner for two' thing. This was a first. I didn't eat all day, in part because of nerves, but also because I wanted to look thin (we've all done it) and so when I drank the enormously extravagant pre-dinner glass of champagne, I instantly felt very unwell. You can guess the rest.

When we met, Ludo was sharing a rented house in South London with his brother and a friend. When I arrived that evening, he answered the door with a tea towel over his shoulder and announced he was preparing dinner. There was no sign of his brother or friend, so they had either been persuaded to go and do something else somewhere else, or had tactfully decided to stay away. I sat at the table with a glass of wine while Ludo poured boiling water into a pan, squeezed a lemon, retrieved a pack of butter from the fridge and put a large chunk of it into another pan. I treasure the memory of this evening for various reasons; watching Ludo cook being one of them. He does cook – he's actually rather good at it, and follows recipes far more assiduously than I do – but it hasn't happened very often since…

Water boils, there's bubbling and steam, the shaking of pans. 'Can you grab a couple of knives and forks?' asks Ludo, nodding towards the drawer where they're kept. 'Almost ready.'

A pan comes off the stove, the water tipped into a waiting colander in the sink. A clatter of plates.

'Here we go.'

In one hand he carries a bowl of what appears to be an awful lot of melted butter and balanced on his other arm are two plates. In the middle of each one sits a globe artichoke.

Ludo spent a large part of his childhood in France, which accounts for his almost flawless French and the fact that he not only knows what a globe artichoke is, but what to do with it. I'm not sure I've ever been in such close proximity to one and I have certainly never attempted eating one. I look down at the curious spiky plant Ludo has placed in front of me and my first thought is how beautiful it is, like a cross between the flower of a waterlily and a large pinecone, with its symmetrical whorl of dark green, scale-like leaves. My second thought is: *how the hell do you eat it?*

Ludo shows me how to detach one of the outside leaves with my fingers, dip its thick, succulent base into the glistening pool of butter and lemon juice, lift it dripping to my mouth and scrape the lemony, buttery bottom of the leaf off with my teeth.

'Oh my god,' I purr, 'how can a bit of tough, boiled leaf taste that good?'

Better still – there are lots of them. It takes a long time to eat an artichoke and it can't and shouldn't be hurried. Every mouthful is to be relished. But what I didn't know was that hidden beneath the protective spikes of its leaves is this beautiful vegetable's heart.

There is now a mound of scraped leaves by each of our plates and what is left is a little pointy pyramid, the shape of a Christmas tree. 'There's nothing much to eat on those, so just pull them off.' I follow his lead and discover that beneath is a tangle of fibres, which Ludo cuts away with his knife. And there is the prize, a thick, pale yellow-green disk. I cut off a chunk and dip it in the dregs of the lemon butter. It is soft, creamy, rich, earthy and indescribably, luxuriously delicious. Never has eating felt so sensuous. Woozy with indulgence, fingers and chins shiny with butter, there is no romantic icebreaker better than eating an artichoke. It worked for us...

*

Now for the flowers. Dahlias, of course, top the list, but to get that lovely, deconstructed look, with plenty to keep my insects happy, Emma suggests Ammi (which look like cow parsley), cornflowers, cosmos, various verbena, scabious, sweet peas and something I'd never heard of called Echinops, but it has purple pompoms, and a purple pompom can never be a bad thing. And euphorbia, because they are her favourite.

'It's going to be amazing!' I say, happily.

'We've got a long way to go between now and amazing,' warns Emma, 'but we have got a plan. You are in charge of getting the vegetable garden clear of weeds and the greenhouse ready, and I'm going to tackle that forest of weeds and overgrown shrubs that is The Bed of Potential Joy. Do I have permission to annihilate the fuchsia?'

Simple Pleasure #4

— A BOWL OF LENTIL STEW ON A DANK DAY —

There is a certain sensation of cold that is hard to banish. It's not the feet-stomping, nose-running chill that makes your fingers tingle and your cheeks burn, that is relieved as soon as you step into a warm room. This is the sensation you get when it's not properly cold outside – it's just dank. And damp. You might want to wear a hat, but you won't miss your gloves. It's not cold enough to merit cranking up the heating once you are indoors, but you become aware, as you sit at your desk, of an unpleasant shiver that starts in the small of the back and works its way very assiduously through your body until it reaches your extremities and even your bones feel cold. The most effective cure I have found to counter this miserable feeling is comfort food and the most comforting of comfort food is, in my mind, lentil stew.

Lentils were – like peas used to be and butter beans still are – on my can't-eat-because-of-their-texture list. But thankfully, with regard to lentils, I have overcome this. And I am truly thankful because lentils are the constituent part of some of my favourite things to eat. Whilst working in Nepal several years ago, I lived on *dal bhat* – the local staple of boiled rice and lentil soup – for a month. I ate it twice a day, every day and I never tired of it. Never once had a hankering or craving to eat anything else. Even when I returned to the UK, the first thing I did was go to the local Nepalese restaurant and order dal bhat, just to get my fix.

Today is one of those dank days. It has been raining all week and I'm damp to the core. Lentil stew is called for. Like skinning a cat, there are many ways to make a lentil stew, and my favourite involves chopping up an onion, a leek, a stick of celery and some garlic and sweating them all in a pan over a low heat until the mixture becomes a soft mush, but not brown. Then there's the spices – a teaspoon each of cumin, cinnamon and paprika. The very fragrance of them as they heat up and mingle with the vegetables starts to make me feel warmer. In goes a dollop of tomato puree, a carrot and a courgette. A bit more sweating and then it's the turn of the lentils. I go for the bigger, sludgy-green-coloured ones. In they go, along with the stock. Salt, chilli flakes, stir. Lid on. It bubbles, in a slightly muddy way, like a volcanic vent, as it stews deliciously. Half an hour and it has become a brown, softly textured gloop that looks wildly unappetizing. But looks, in this case, are immaterial. Spoon a generous ladle or two into a bowl, top it with a dollop of plain yoghurt and some coriander leaves if you're feeling fancy, then wrap your hands around the warmth of the bowl and lift it to your face so you can breathe in its earthy, spicy, deeply comforting aroma. Then eat. And tell me it doesn't warm your cockles.

*

FEELING KNEADY
*

I'm one of those people that finds cooking therapeutic. That doesn't mean that there aren't plenty of occasions when I get home after a long day and wish dinner could magically appear on the table. And there are also those times when I can't summon the energy to do more than put a slice of bread in the toaster or eat an apple. But generally, the gentle routine of gathering a few raw ingredients, combining them and cooking them is something I take great pleasure in. I use recipes – reading cookbooks can be almost as good as eating – sometimes following them to the letter, but more often than not, just for inspiration. But my usual approach to cooking is to see what's in the fridge and make something up. A small creative challenge that's not over-taxing. And the chopping, stirring, pouring and sprinkling that follows is mindless enough to be soothing, but not so mindless as to be boring. What I can't abide is faffing about with food, juggling long lists of ingredients, gadgetry and processes just to turn something into a foam or a smear. If the ingredients are good enough to eat, you shouldn't have to do a lot to them is my philosophy.

I learned to cook with my mum. I don't remember her ever actually teaching me. I just helped in the kitchen and picked things up that way. And for my tenth birthday I was given my first recipe book by my grandfather – I can still picture the cover and the illustrations – and I learned how to make things like cheese on toast and chocolate fudge. The glow of pride I felt when someone ate something I'd made and declared it delicious (as they kindly, but perhaps not always honestly, did) was intoxicating.

My childhood culinary references were limited. Growing up in a fairly rural area in the 70s meant eating out was something we just didn't do. We had the occasional holiday in a hotel and would eat in the restaurant there, the memorable start to breakfast being when the waiter would ask, 'Would you like orange juice or half a grapefruit?' – you could have either, but not both – but generally we stayed in self-catering cottages. I was well into my teens before I went to a restaurant, just for one evening, to eat out.

It was an occasion, a treat to celebrate a birthday or something like that. My grandfather was taking us and had chosen a Chinese restaurant in his local town. We sat at a round table, with a heavy white cloth and napkins. There were chopsticks which, to my mind, seemed ill-designed for transporting food from plate to mouth. And I had never seen or tasted anything like the plates of food that arrived and were put in the middle of the table for us to share. Mum's staples were things like shepherd's pie (and no one makes a better one), cauliflower cheese and Lancashire hotpot – homely and delicious. The things that have become so commonplace now, like avocados and sweet potatoes, I didn't taste or even see until I was an adult. But my abiding memory of the evening in the Chinese restaurant was picking out a green bean from a bowl of otherwise unidentifiable things and eating it. Within a second or two my head felt as if it was on fire, my nose started to run, my eyes to burn and water. Unbeknownst to me, I'd eaten a whole chilli. Again, something I'd never seen or tasted before. It is perhaps curious that I didn't develop a lifelong aversion to them as a result – the opposite is true.

Making pastry and baking were not big parts of Mum's culinary repertoire. She could knock up a very reasonable Victoria sponge for birthdays – she used to make one flavoured with orange zest that was my favourite – but otherwise we didn't cook or eat a great deal in the way of cakes or puddings. As a consequence, I don't make them very much now either. And, even if I slavishly follow a recipe, it is rarely a success. But I would have loved to learn to make bread. Mum may refute this, but I don't remember her ever even attempting to make it. The bread we ate, with, I'm sorry to admit, the crusts cut off ('the best bit!' I now admonish Mum, who still cuts them off), was a brown loaf delivered along with two pints of milk in clinking glass bottles by the milkman.

Bread is almost as intrinsic to human civilization as walking upright on two legs. Even before the advent of agriculture, our hunter-gatherer ancestors were making and eating bread. At an archaeological site in Jordan, the charred crumbs of a flatbread made from wild wheat, barley and roots were found to date back to some time between 14,600 and 11,600 years ago. Once wheat was domesticated around 10,000 years ago in the Fertile Crescent – a part of the world that gave rise to the advancement of almost every area of human knowledge – bread became central to the formation of early human societies. And now, thousands of years later, it remains a staple throughout much of the world.

I had the privilege – and it really was a privilege – to live for a number of weeks alongside the people of the Wakhi tribe in the very north-east of Afghanistan. These remarkable people who live and eke out a way of life at altitudes of between 3,000 and 5,000 metres are amongst the poorest in the world. And their lives, farming tiny pockets of stony land with a growing season of barely three months, and battling to keep their livestock alive through the long and brutal winters, are unimaginably hard, something which is reflected in their life expectancy of a mere

35 years. But as is so often the case with people who have so little, they are generous, kind and hospitable, treating strangers as members of the family.

Their meagre diet consists primarily of two things – tea and bread. Milk from their sheep and goats is boiled over a smoking fire on the earth floor of their small stone houses. A few precious tea leaves are thrown in and a spoonful of sugar and it is poured into small, thick glass tumblers or an assortment of old tin mugs. The bread is made, several flat loaves at a time, from a basic mix of coarse flour, salt and water. As far as I recall, yeast wasn't used. The dough was scooped out of the bowl by the handful, rolled into shape and then flattened into a rough circle and baked on the hot stones at the edge of the fire.

My first morning I got up at dawn and, with the mother of the family and her two teenage daughters, went to milk the goats and sheep. We were staying at their summer camp – a thousand or more metres above their permanent valley home. During the short summers the animals are walked up here to these high-altitude pastures so that crops can be grown in the valley below. I'm here in late August but already, in the early morning, before the sun has had a chance to warm the earth, it is below freezing. As we walk to the stone enclosure where the sheep spend the night to protect them from predators, our breath steams and our cold fingers reach gratefully beneath the warm, woolly bellies as we start to milk. It takes the four of us a long time – probably two hours – and when we're finished and the sheep have been loosed out into the hills, we are stiff with cold and very hungry. Tea and bread may not sound like much of a breakfast, but to gather around the fire with a mug of sweet, smoky tea and a hunk of bread almost too hot to eat was pure luxury.

The deep, satisfying comfort of fresh, warm bread is synonymous for me with David Wilson's kitchen. David Wilson is a farmer. He is also a skilled and inveterate bread maker. His kitchen is full of sourdough baskets and the intoxicating smell of freshly baked bread. When I go to see him, we sit at the long kitchen table with a pot of coffee and the loaf David has made that morning. This is not his customary sourdough. It is a rich, dark bread, but when I bite into it, it doesn't have the heavy, dense texture of rye and it tastes slightly nutty.

'Mmmm,' I mumble appreciatively between mouthfuls, 'this is delicious. Is it some funny grain I've never heard of?'

David shakes his head. 'No, it's wheat. But just not the variety we've all become accustomed to.'

As human populations have grown and become more urbanized, there is ever increasing pressure to produce food to keep the world fed. The big-scale agriculture that has developed to meet this challenge has meant that high yields, resistance to disease and pests, convenience and profit are more important than what is good in the long term, not just for the planet but also for us – the ones who eat it. And wheat is a perfect example.

Wild wheat – *Triticum boeoticum* – still grows in parts of the Middle East and the Balkans. It is shorter than cultivated wheat and not very productive. When we domesticated it, as we did with all the plants and animals we consume, we started to tinker with it, selectively breeding it so the stems grew to a uniform length (which made it easier to reap with modern machinery) and it produced more grains. This selective breeding gave us the ability to control, as much as we possibly could, the success of our harvest each year. We wanted guarantees. But nature doesn't offer guarantees. She is fickle that way. And so we've tried to cheat her and outsmart her, particularly as far as wheat is concerned.

Wheat is the world's most widely grown crop. Upwards of 700 million tonnes are produced from over 200 million hectares throughout Europe, Asia, North and South America. In the last 50 years the area where wheat is sown has doubled and the yield per hectare has tripled. It is also the world's most widely traded food grain. We rely, almost exclusively, on two selectively bred species: durum wheat, which accounts for 5 per cent of all wheat produced, and common or bread wheat, which makes up the remaining 95 per cent.

To get flour from wheat, the grains are separated from the rest of the plant and ground. Traditionally this was done by stone milling, but now almost all the flour we buy, or that is used in foods we buy, is milled through steel rollers. Steel roller mills were developed in the 1870s and revolutionized grain milling. They could produce much finer white flour much more quickly than stone milling and, as a consequence, wheat flour became cheaper. But at a cost. When a grain is milled through metal rollers, two elements of the grain are lost. One is the bran, which provides the fibre, protein and vitamins that are vital for maintaining a healthy digestive system. The other is the germ, which provides B vitamins and fatty acids that are also beneficial to our health. What is left is the endosperm and it is the endosperm that contains all the glutens.

The vast majority of the wheat grown throughout the world, and incorporated into so much of what we eat, is milled in a manner that robs it of important nutrients but retains a level of glutens not found in traditional wheat or grain varieties. Common wheat contains a very high proportion of Triticeae glutens – the sticky substance that allows dough to rise and retain its shape during baking. But those glutens are also useful added to other foods and so many of the things we eat, particularly if they are processed, contain them. Our bodies are regularly challenged to digest a diet containing more glutens than ever in our human history, which is why intolerances to gluten and the diseases associated with them have increased so dramatically in recent years. But our over-dependency on this single crop may have even more dire consequences. Because it has been discovered that common wheat is highly susceptible to climate change. In a study published in the journal *Nature* in 2016, it was shown that rising temperatures are going to have a dramatic and detrimental effect on wheat production and the world food supply. You can't outsmart nature for ever.

The farm David manages is a mixed organic farm of around 1,000 acres. His guiding principle is sustainability, not just for the long-term health of the land and the wildlife it supports (which also benefits the farm), but, like any business, the farm needs to be financially sustainable too. So he still strives to get good crop yields and to raise livestock in a way that is cost effective, but working with nature, rather than against her. He trials ways of using the land to make it more productive and efficient – agri-forestry is one example, where vegetable crops are grown alongside fruit trees. But his overriding concern, the thing the world needs to address with increasing urgency, is the dependency it has on this one variety of wheat that is now in peril. So David has started to track down old, heritage varieties, testing them out to see how well they grow, how they cope with pests or diseases and unpredictable weather. He wants to know how they affect the soil, and of course, how they taste. He has a flour mill in his kitchen. It is about the size of a coffee machine and beside it is a bowl of grains grown in the fields around the house. The bread I'm eating now is made from wheat that was sown, tended, harvested and milled by David himself. You don't get much more artisan than that.

I have frequent pangs of regret that I don't make bread – well, not by hand. For many years we've had a bread machine, and unlike many of them, which end up unused and covered in spiders' webs in attics and garages, we use ours all the time. The bread we eat, we make. But there is no skill involved. Although its taste and texture is infinitely superior to supermarket bread, I don't look at the loaf I shake out of the tin, once the machine has magically transformed the ingredients I tipped into it, unmixed and untouched, with any sort of pride. I have – literally – had no hand in its making. I did attempt to make bread properly, once. In a flurry of enthusiasm inspired by I'm not sure what, I found and followed to the letter a Delia Smith recipe. One she claimed couldn't fail, but she underestimated me. I baked a brick. I couldn't even taste it because no knife I owned would get through it. I'd have needed a chainsaw.

My visit to David inspired me to have another go. Again, I chose a failsafe recipe. I measured out the ingredients with the utmost care, even weighing the water, which, the recipe stated, was the way to ensure you had exactly the required amount. 'And don't worry if your dough seems a bit wet.' I poured the water into the bowl with the dry ingredients and started to mix them together. Almost instantly my fingers and hands were entangled in a sticky, gluey mess of flour and water that defiantly refused to form into a beautifully soft, pliant ball of dough as the recipe promised it would. Instead it got stickier and stickier and more and more impossible to work. There was more dough stuck to my hands than there was in the bowl. Eventually I scraped what I could into a sort of ball and left it, as instructed, under a tea towel on the back of the kitchen range to rise.

I wasn't overly optimistic when I lifted the corner of the tea towel after the prescribed hour or so and peeped into the bowl. But to my utter amazement the sorry-looking lump I had left had risen beautifully.

'Bloody hell!' I muttered incredulously, and tipped it out on to a floured worktop to, slightly regretfully, knock it back. Back it went, under its cloth and once again defied expectation and rose. I lifted it with due reverence and placed it on an oiled baking tray, put two slashes in the top with a knife as instructed and slid it into the oven.

When I lifted up the finished result, I realized I had spent an entire morning making something that bore an uncanny resemblance to a cowpat and was all but inedible. Clearly breadmaking is beyond me. But it was a failure that niggled. I didn't really want to accept it. And although experience told me that making bread is anything but simple, I couldn't dissuade myself from thinking that simplicity and bread-making are somehow synonymous with each other. For that is the beauty of bread, the thing that has given it its enduring appeal: a few very basic ingredients, the hands-on manipulating of those ingredients that is (or can be) almost meditative, the enforced pause while nature and chemistry do their thing, the baking, and a tangible, edible result that is made to share.

I'm pinning my hopes on Jennifer. Her website, Dough & Daughters, makes the rather rash claim that everyone can learn to make bread: it just takes information, practice and confidence.

'It is all about mastering the dough,' she tells me, as she hands me an apron, 'not letting it master you. People always fear the results, think of bread as some sort of monster that is going to overpower them, but once you're in control, once you've taken charge, your bread will be perfect every time.'

I give her a doubtful look and hold up my phone.

'This is a photo of the last loaf of bread I made,' I said, showing her the cowpat.

Jennifer gives it a dismissive wave of her hand. 'Let's get started.'

We are in the kitchen of her old, very beautiful cottage tucked up amongst the green and heathery slopes of the Black Mountains. On the wooden table beneath the timbered ceiling are metal bowls, wooden boards, jugs and a set of scales.

'I grew up on a farm,' Jennifer tells me – she is the daughter of a Danish mother and Cuban father and her childhood was spent in southern Spain – 'and we were encouraged to cook, but it was all rather trial and error. I used to bake like Miss Piggy – sling in a bit of this and a bit of that. But you can't do that with bread. It is all about precision. One of the mistakes people always make is to think, "Oh, my dough's a bit sticky, I'll add more flour", or "It's a bit dry" and pour in more water. But you need to make bread with the mindset of a scientist.'

At this point I wonder if I should leave, rather than waste Jennifer's time, because precision is not something that comes naturally to me in any area of my life. And then she takes out of the oven a loaf of Scandinavian raisin and caraway bread she made before I arrived. It looks like a work of art and fills the kitchen with wafts of spicy, fruity fragrance. One day, I resolve to myself, I'm going to get good enough to make that. So I tie the apron around my waist and we wash our hands at the sink.

We are going to make a basic white loaf. Jennifer has already weighed out 500g of organic white flour in a bowl and she instructs me to weigh out exactly 10g of sea salt and pour it into the flour on one side of the bowl and break off 10g of fresh yeast and crumble it into the other side. 'The salt should never mix with the yeast outside the flour,' she says. 'That's why you introduce them on opposite sides of the bowl. The salt will kill the active ingredients in the yeast and your bread won't rise.' I've never used fresh yeast before. It comes in a soft, brown block that flakes when it is cut. And it has a wonderful smell, slightly sour and mushroomy, but hard to define. 'Umami,' we decide.

We weigh out 350g of water in a jug.

'My grandmother taught me that weighing water was essential to making bread,' Jennifer says, watching the needle on my scales to make sure I am precise enough. 'That's good. Right, tip it into the flour. Now, this is the point people get scared because their hands get sticky and messy and they don't feel able to work the dough properly.'

'That's exactly the problem,' I say, recalling the hopelessness I felt when I tried to mix the dough last time.

But Jennifer keeps one hand on the rim of the bowl and in the other she holds a dough scraper – 'the most useful tool' – and she shows me how she uses it to incorporate the water and flour, gently scraping along the side of the bowl and folding the ingredients together.

'You need to stand with your feet slightly ajar, one foot in front of the other and relax, because you are going to move with the dough, it is almost a rocking motion.'

She tells me how she visited a bakery in Havana and the stone floor was worn down exactly in the spots where the bakers stood to mix their dough.

'A lot of people think that dough has to be kneaded, but in essence that is the wrong approach, because it knocks the air out of it. By mixing it this way, we create pockets of air, which is what we want.'

We stand by side by side, rocking back and forth, and before long the mix in Jennifer's bowl has become smooth and pliable, but mine still looks like badly mixed cement.

'Don't lose faith,' she admonishes me. 'It is coming together whatever you think.'

And she was right. Not long afterwards, I had something that looked passably like dough.

We tipped the mixture out of the bowls and on to wooden boards.

'No flour?' I asked.

'You don't need it, you've got your scraper, and remember the need for precision. You don't want to add any more flour to the mix, even a little bit.'

She shows me how to pick up the top of the dough using just the tips of my fingers, to keep the heat of my hands away from it; lift it, allowing gravity to stretch it; then slap it down and fold it over. The action is repeated, taking the dough from the side. When bits of dough stick to the board, Jennifer instructs me to scoop the dough lightly into my hand with the scraper and then scrape the board and carry on lifting, slapping down and folding. Jennifer does this with the practised rhythm and deftness of someone who has been making bread since she was a child. Her grandmother taught her and it was, she said, just something she and her siblings did if they were at a loose end. 'We'd just go into the kitchen and make bread.'

I'm finding it difficult to ease into the rhythm. I'll get it, then lose it again.

'Just relax. Don't let the dough get away from you. You're in charge.'

I'm still making heavy work of it, but Jennifer is infinitely patient and gradually the movements start to come together, to feel more natural and intuitive. My dough sticks to the board far more than Jennifer's, but this, she tells me, is just because she can work more quickly.

'It comes with practice, like anything. If you make a loaf of bread every weekend, you'll soon get the feel for it, and when you do, it is wonderfully therapeutic. I love the sound of the dough slapping down on the board.'

My dough is becoming more elastic and springy in texture. 'My grandmother used to tell us that the dough was ready "when it looks like the belly of a nun that has never seen the sun"'!'

I look at the soft mound of dough on Jennifer's board and it does, with a bit of imagination, look like a little pale pot belly. Mine still needs rather more imagination, but with Jennifer's encouragement I keep going, picking it up, stretching it, slapping it down, folding it over.

'Oh, look,' she says delightedly, 'it's almost there!'

We leave our 'nuns' bellies' to prove for an hour and Jennifer shows me how to make another loaf – this one, she tells me, involves no yeast and needs no kneading.

'It's a great quick fix if you haven't got any bread and you need to make some quickly. It's similar to Irish soda bread, but this is a Danish recipe made with oats and treacle.'

Even I had to concede that making this bread was easy. Flour, oats and bicarbonate of soda are mixed together in a bowl, to which is added either buttermilk or a mix of yoghurt and milk, and 100ml of boiling water into which has been melted three generous tablespoons of black treacle. Then you simply get a big spoon and stir the whole lot up. 'You're aiming for a brown mush,' said Jennifer, 'there's no other way to describe it. It's not going to look like a nun's tummy. This is going to be a much rougher, more textured dough.' Once again, I seem to have made a cowpat, but this time, that is what it should look like. We put slits in the top 'to let the fairies out' – vital when making soda bread, apparently. If you don't, they jinx it, and I want to give mine every chance of working.

Afterwards, I leave Jennifer's house to go and have lunch with a friend who lives nearby. 'I hope you've brought the bread,' she says when I arrive, 'because I haven't got any left in the house at all.' I hold up the paper bags into which Jennifer has put the two white loaves and the wonderfully dark, aromatic treacle loaf I made. I feel ridiculously pleased with myself. I know it will take a lot of practice to be able to make bread the way Jennifer does, as if it were second nature, but I do now have the belief that I am capable of making bread and not just bricks or cowpats. And perhaps one day I will find myself saying, as Jennifer did when I thanked her profusely for her time and endless patience, 'I just love making bread. I never tire of it. If I'm feeling down, or exhausted, or I've been dealing with a lot of stress at work, I come home and make bread. It's the simple cure for everything.'

Simple Pleasure #5
— TOAST, BUTTER, MARMITE —

Toast. Student staple, comfort food, rescue remedy for those too exhausted to cook, or those that don't know how to cook. Forgiving (burn it and it can be fixed with a bit of judicious scraping) and endlessly adaptable. The simple act of toasting (I don't think I can go as far as to call it an art) transforms one of those flabby, scrawny coffee-shop sandwiches that come in a plastic envelope into, if not an

Epicurean treat, then at least something with texture, even if it entirely lacks taste. A bit of crunch can make eating the blandest of dishes a bit more exciting. Look at Rice Krispies.

The thickness of a piece of toast matters, and it does rather depend on what it is being used for. Toast for breakfast, or a snack, needs to be a robust slice, not thin and floppy. So ideally it should be from a loaf that needs slicing by hand. Our bread-maker bread makes really good toast, although nothing beats my friend Polly's sourdough. Maybe my fledgling bread-making skills will one day make a loaf that surpasses even that, but I suspect it will be a while. Everyone has a preference for how toasted they like their toast to be. Personally, I like it well browned, and if the thickness of the slice is right, there is then a perfect crunch-to-squish ratio. What has to be avoided is through and through crispness, which just ends up as crumbs, and provides none of the comforting stodge that makes toast so universally appealing.

Then there is the bewildering number of things that go with toast, although I will never sully a slice with either chocolate or sandwich spread. Ludo's homemade marmalade is a strong contender for top toast topper, as is his cheese on toast recipe, which involves beating an egg, grating strong cheddar into it, mixing it all up with Lea and Perrins Worcestershire Sauce and salt and pepper, piling it generously onto a piece of toast and putting it under the grill. But my go-to, never-fails-to-satisfy choice is butter (and it must be butter, salted at that) and Marmite. I'm not going to make a case for Marmite. We all know you either love it or hate it, and lovers of it don't need telling that its pungent, yeasty saltiness is irresistible. What I have never understood, though, is Marmite lovers who only love it if it is so thinly applied it almost isn't there. Like the butter beneath it, it needs to be spread generously, covering the toast in a glossy, dark slick. There is literally nothing better to sink your teeth into.

That said, there is a strong case for crumpets too. Put Marmite and butter on those and the two mix deliciously and seep down through the crumpet's permeable surface, infusing it with that wonderfully savoury butteriness. But I'm not going to attempt to make those until I'm confident with my 'belly of a nun'.

*

Make Do
and Mend

OLD BOOTS
*

As I tie my laces this morning, I look ruefully at the boot I've just put on my left foot. It has a hole in it. I've had these boots for a good long time, and they've carried me for many miles. I've been resisting getting a new pair, partly because the hole started out as pretty small and insignificant and partly because they are so comfortable, and I feel an odd sort of loyalty towards them. But now the hole is getting bigger, my sock clearly visible through it, and the soles of both boots are worn and starting to come away from the uppers. The time has probably come to replace them. And it'll be easy to do it. When I get back from my walk I can go online and get the same make, possibly even the same model, sent out to arrive the next day. But somehow that doesn't seem right. For something as important to me as walking boots, not only do I want to try them on, make sure they feel right, I also think I will appreciate them more and care for them better if I have at least made the effort to go out and physically find them and take time choosing the right pair.

Online shopping for anything from footwear and food to furniture is now the way that many of us acquire what we need or want. Almost no one, it seems, is immune from the lure and convenience of buying stuff via the internet. Amazon, in its quest to fill the world with warehouses, delivery drivers and drones, will even send out goods to people living in remote villages in rural India. And if they don't have a bank account (and most of them don't), they simply pay cash on delivery.

Buying stuff via the internet should be ideal for me – I don't enjoy shopping, get panicked in malls and the concept of retail ever being considered 'therapy' is incomprehensible. And I do buy things online, but I'm becoming increasingly aware that it makes me feel uncomfortable and sort of guilty. It is such a mindless, careless way to shop. Disengaged and remote. And I feel mutinous when 'If you've bought this, you might also like this...' pops up on the screen. I suppose it is no different than a person working behind the till asking, 'Would you like a giant bar of chocolate or a muffin wrapped in plastic to go with your newspaper?' but you know they are offering the same thing to everyone they serve. They are not pretending to read your mind. When a computer thinks it knows what I might desire, it feels like an invasion of privacy.

I wonder, too, whether the ease and remoteness of shopping online – sitting at a desk, or on a sofa, or on the bus, scrolling through pictures on a screen, clicking a button a few times – makes us buy more stuff than we need and care about it less. At the risk of being one of those people who say, with a slightly sad shake of the head, 'It wasn't like that in my day', I'm going to hark back to my childhood again. I had what I imagine was a fairly typical middle-class upbringing for the time. My dad worked, Mum stayed at home and looked after me and my brother and all the domestic duties that go with caring for a house and a family. We were given pocket money (a few pence a week) and could also earn extra by doing things like cleaning Dad's car or helping in the garden.

We had piggy banks and if we wanted something (in my case, it was usually something to do with a horse – a hoof pick or a new headcollar, although when I discovered ABBA I knew life wouldn't be complete without the single of 'Mamma Mia'), we had to save up. And when we had enough money, the trip to go and buy whatever it was we had saved so hard to get was all part of the excitement.

I remember to this day the rush of anticipation as I ran across the nylon carpet tiles of WH Smith to the area where the singles were, lined up in racks, numbered according to their position in the charts that week. Anxiously carrying the plastic disk in its paper cover to the till and handing over a handful of hot coins that had been clenched in my fist since we left home. The coins would be counted, and I would hold my breath and not breathe again until the disk was put in a bag and handed back to me. I would clutch that bag as if it were the most precious thing on earth and skip back across the carpet tiles, flush with the sense of achievement that comes from working and saving and waiting. I had earned my ABBA single and now I could and would really enjoy it. Again and again and again. My poor parents...

Up until a few weeks ago I would have gone to my friend Matt's shop to get a new pair of boots. It was one of the few shops I really enjoyed going to. The big, airy space wasn't crammed with stuff, in the way that some shops seem to think is appealing and I find overwhelming and off-putting. Instead it felt like a carefully curated selection of gear chosen by someone with a genuine passion for the outdoors. Matt and the people who worked with him also understood that what they were selling was something of an investment for the people buying. Good-quality boots, waterproof coats, merino thermals, tents and sleeping bags are not fashion items to use for a season and then discard. They are expensive and built to last. I've got things I've been wearing or using for years, but I always take advice before I buy. I don't want to be swayed by colour or label, but to be reassured I am getting the best bit of kit for the job. I want to be able to talk to someone, take advantage of their experience and expertise. And in an era when so many people say they feel lonely, shops like Matt's, with its friendly approachable staff and its little café amidst the racks of fleeces, bobble hats and climbing gear, where you could sit with a coffee and a wickedly large slice of cake and swap travel stories with other customers, should be doing great business. There's no friendly advice or 'welcome back' banter when you shop online, even if you are a loyal customer who has shopped via a particular site many times before. But Matt's shop couldn't compete with cheaper online prices and limitless choice. It seems not enough of us valued his expertise, the time he would spend making sure what we were buying was right and that it fitted perfectly. Not enough people chose to support the enterprise of a hard-working, ever-inventive individual who did everything he could to help his customers whether they were regulars or not. Instead they went online, embraced the impersonal, faceless click-to-buy-now form of shopping, had the fleeting satisfaction of getting something a bit cheaper. And I think it is this that has been niggling away at my conscience and is at the root of the discomfort I feel when I shop online.

I get my replacement boots in a shop, not quite as local as Matt's, but not too far away. And, like Matt's shop was, this one is independently owned and run by people who love the outdoors and use the same kit they sell. That unbiased, tried-and-tested knowledge is the thing I appreciate most and is the reason I will drive for 45 minutes to get to their shop, rather than go online. Nothing is more reassuring, or indeed persuasive, than personal recommendation. It is why today's online 'influencers' have become such a powerful commodity for retailers and manufacturers. But how much influencing would they be willing to do, I wonder, if they weren't being paid? Do they genuinely rate the products they peddle to their insatiable followers, or are they only as *fabulous* and *must-have* as the money they are promised with every sale?

What I should have done, of course, as soon as that first hole started to open up in my boot and the tread of the soles started wearing thin, was to find out if they could be repaired. They weren't leather boots, so it may not have been possible, but I could have at least enquired. That said, I'm not sure where I would have gone to find out. The cobbler's shop in our local town, probably. It shares a premises with the dry cleaners and offers key-cutting as well as resoling and they'll nail those little metal plates on to the worn-down heels of shoes, making the wearer sound like an unskilled tap-dancer. But I'm not sure they undertake anything more intricate than that. And no one probably asks them to, because repairing things is no longer the default solution when something breaks or wears out. We just throw whatever it is away and buy a new one.

In 2018 the *Economist* ran an article with the headline 'Repair is as Important as Innovation'. Its author had attended The Festival of Maintenance in London. It was the first of what is now an annual non-profit event run by volunteers and is, its website explains, 'a celebration of those who maintain different parts of our world, and how they do it, recognizing the often hidden work done in repair, custodianship, stewardship, tending and caring for things that matter'.

In the article, the writer makes the observation that 'events about making new things are ten a penny. Less common are events about keeping things as good as new. Maintenance,' he writes, insightfully, 'lacks the glamour of innovation.' One of the speakers was David Edgerton, a historian of science and technology and 20th-century Britain at King's College London, and he made the point that 'maintenance is often dismissed as mere drudgery. But in fact, repairing things is often trickier than making them.' And I suspect Martine Postma would agree with him.

CALL ME OLD-FASHIONED
*

'Dammit!' growls Ludo, taking two, flabby, very un-toasted bits of bread out of the toaster. 'Bloody thing's broken.' We've had that toaster a long time, perhaps even before we moved to Wales, which was more than a decade ago. It's one of those hefty metal ones with a mechanical timer you twist as far as you want your toast brown, and levers to lower the slices of bread into its hot maw and raise them back up again when they're done. Except today the maw is distinctly chilly.

'I'll order a new one.'

'It's probably just the element,' I say, as if I know what I'm talking about. Which I don't. 'Can't they just be replaced?'

I'm quibbling about automatically chucking out the old toaster and getting a new one, not because I have a strange affection for it (although as toasters go, it has a chunky, no-nonsense aesthetic that is rather pleasing and it has toasted faithfully every morning for a long time), but because of an article I read in a Malaysian newspaper. It was about a new kind of café that had recently started up in Kuala Lumpur. As you'd expect from a café, it served coffee and snacks, but there's nothing newsworthy about that. This café had made the national press because people were flocking to it, not for cake, but to get things repaired. Lamps. Clothing. Radios. Anything, in fact, portable enough to get through the door. The people doing the repairs had volunteered their time; men and women with tools, sewing machines and skills that they were all too happy to share. The repairs were collaborative; the owners of the broken items encouraged to learn how to take it apart, where dirt might clog a pipe, how to change a fuse or patch a pair of jeans. And as well as being practical, learning to fix things had proved to be social too. Fun, even. It was such a success, more cafés like it were being planned in other parts of the city.

The idea of a repair café didn't originate in Malaysia, nor is it the only one. There are nearly two thousand of them now and they are all over the world. There's even one in Abergavenny, not far from where I live. But the first repair café opened in Holland, in Amsterdam, and it came about because of one woman by the name of Martine Postma. She wasn't famous, or rich, or well connected. She was just an ordinary person who grew up making clothes for her dolls and wishing she was Laura Ingalls Wilder from *Little House on the Prairie*.

I love stories like this; stories of people who just get on and do things, without being hamstrung by the potential for difficulties or failure. I wondered if I could go and meet Martine, find out more, and emailed the Repair Café Foundation to ask. I waited a week, but there was no reply. So I did something wildly old-fashioned and phoned instead. A woman answered and I asked if I could speak to Martine Postma.

'I'm Martine,' she replied. She was friendly, efficient. She had got my email but had had a busy week and hadn't got around to replying. 'I'm happy for you to interview me via Skype,' she suggested.

'Would you mind very much if I came to meet you in person?' I ventured. 'I'd like to see the café too and perhaps talk to some of the volunteers.'

There was a pause.

'The thing is,' Martine said eventually, sounding slightly embarrassed, 'I would really rather you didn't come by plane.'

I took a train to London and another to Amsterdam. I could have flown. On paper, it was more convenient and cheaper, but the truth is,

I just didn't consider any other way of getting to Holland. It was Martine's environmental concerns that made her request I didn't fly over in order to meet her, and that's why I looked for an alternative. And instead of being the stressful, harried journey that short-haul flights so often are, the trip by train was calm and rather restful. I enjoyed the sense of really travelling, of seeing the landscape pass by the window. When I arrived at the station, there was no hanging about waiting for luggage, no trying to find the right bus, or train, or queue for a taxi. I just walked out into the sunshine and half an hour later I was at my hotel.

The hotel had bicycles to rent, and cycling proved to be absolutely the best way to get around Amsterdam. It's flat – which helps when you haven't ridden a bike for a while – and safe, because there are dedicated, clearly marked bike-only lanes everywhere. No one, I notice, as I pedal towards the community hall where I'm meeting Martine, wears a helmet.

Martine's just finishing up a meeting when I arrive, so I go and chat to John, who is wrestling with Kim's coffee machine.

'Getting into it without breaking it is the most difficult thing,' he says, through gritted teeth. 'Repairing it is the easy part.' It's Kim's first time at a repair café. I ask her why she's come.

'It is quite an expensive machine and it was working until last week, so I don't think it is a big problem. But it's not under guarantee any more, so I thought I would try and get it fixed here. I didn't want to just throw it away without at least seeing if it could be repaired.'

'That's why I'm here,' says John, with a triumphant smile, having just managed to prise open the machine and reveal its workings. 'It's a sort of rebellion against all those companies that make goods that they know will break down just after the guarantee runs out. They do their best to stop people repairing them, using screws like these' (and he holds up an odd, oval-shaped screw to show me) 'that need a special tool. But it can be almost impossible to get that tool. And then they offer a 20 per cent discount if you buy a new one, so that's what people do and the old one just gets thrown away. It is so wasteful. I hate it.'

It was also Martine's hatred of waste that was the genesis of the idea for the cafés. We get a coffee and sit opposite each other at a table. She is tall, slim, in skirt and trainers, and I guess about the same age as me. Articulate and precise, she is clearly used to being interviewed, but still she gives thoughtful consideration to each question I ask. Before she came up with the concept of a repair café, she worked as an environmental journalist and it was waste reduction that seemed, to her, the key to a more sustainable way of life for everyone. An apparently simple way to reduce waste is to make existing products last longer; repair them rather than throw them away. But it turns out it's not that simple.

'People don't repair things any more because they don't know how to do it. They don't have the skills or the tools, they don't have the time, and in many cases it is cheaper and easier to get something new than to get an old item repaired,' Martine tells me. What was needed, she reasoned, was a new way of thinking: give people the impetus to find out whether something could be fixed rather than automatically throwing it away. 'I wanted the idea of repair to be as normal as getting a new product, but I knew it would only work if it was as cheap and easy to get something fixed, and also more fun.' She tested the concept by hiring a room at her local theatre. She persuaded her friend's husband (the only person she knew who could repair things) to be one of the volunteers. The others she found by asking around the community. Many of the people who signed up were in their sixties and seventies. 'They were really happy to join in and help, to feel useful again and share their skills.'

That first event made it clear to Martine that it shouldn't just be a one-off.

'People were asking if they could come back the following week; they had other things that needed fixing. But I think it was the fact that it was fun, it was social and it was local that was its greater appeal.'

The following year she set up the Repair Café Foundation with the long-term plan of establishing a network of twelve repair cafés, one in each province of the Netherlands. Twelve swiftly became fifty, the media got wind of the story and the repair-café movement was being talked about all over the world. But better still, it captured the imagination of the public. People living outside the Netherlands wanted their own repair cafés.

'So we put together a manual, a sort of starter kit, and made it available on our website, telling people how to set up their own. It's been translated into seven different languages now.'

The Foundation is ten years old and Martine is still very much at the helm.

'This is my lifestyle. It doesn't even feel like work. It's just my dream.'

Does she have a long-term plan? Her answer takes me by surprise.

'The success of the repair cafés is a sign that something is missing. As social events, where neighbours can help each other fix beloved items, they are great, but that shouldn't be the only way to get things repaired. It should be possible for a professional repair man or woman to earn a decent living offering that service. The problem is that labour is taxed very highly and raw materials are hardly taxed at all. In Western societies, goods can be produced more cheaply than paying someone to repair them. And until that changes, people will keep buying cheap stuff and throwing it away, creating enormous amounts of waste and polluting the earth. If the way taxes were levied was changed, if goods were to become a little more expensive but the labour to repair them was cheaper, we wouldn't need repair cafés. You could get anything repaired anywhere. That would be my ideal.'

It may sound like a pipe dream, but there are signs that societies and the people who govern them are starting to consider the old-fashioned concept of repairing in a new light. In March 2019 California became the 20th American state to consider the Right to Repair Bill. The bill requires companies to allow consumers access to parts and service information. A spokesman for US PIRG (the federation of state Public Interest Research Groups that works on behalf of the American public on issues connected with health and well-being) said: 'People just want to fix their stuff. We are tired of manufacturers price-gouging for repairs, selling us disposable electronics and pushing us to buy new instead of fixing what we already have...Electronic waste is the fastest-growing waste stream in the world. It's high time we stopped manufacturers from blocking repair, which keeps devices working and off the scrap heap. It's better for consumers and better for the environment, and whether or not manufacturers like it, more and more people agree. We deserve the right to repair our products.'

Ludo sighs, turns the toaster upside-down, scattering months' worth of crumbs, and finds the serial number. The new elements arrive a couple of days later. He dons a head torch, lays out his tools like a surgeon and sits on the sofa with the toaster on a tray on his knees. At each stage of the disassembly he takes photos on his phone to remind him how to put everything back together. I make lots of encouraging comments and admiring noises, which I think is crucial to the eventual outcome. Four hours and quite a lot of cursing later, the toaster is plugged back in. Ludo twists the mechanical timer and the elements start to glow.

'You're brilliant!' I say.

'Humph,' he replies, but he can't hide a small smile of triumph.

There is, of course, another way to reduce the number of electronic gadgets that end up in landfill. This story was recalled by Elmo Stoll, one of the contributors to the collection of essays in *The Plain Reader*. It made me smile.

Better Than Fixing Things
A man from a big city moved to a house in the countryside,
right in the middle of a community of plain people (which is
the way they refer to themselves). The big city man was a little
apprehensive about finding himself surrounded by people who
travelled by horse and cart, and chose to have no power lines
connected to their buildings. But on the day he moved in, one of
his new neighbours arrived at his house, unasked, to help him
unload his belongings. And he proved very useful, strong as he
was from farm work and manual labour. He helped carry into
the city man's house his array of electrical appliances, labour-
saving machines and gadgets. And when he'd unloaded them all
and put them in the house, he said to the city man, 'If any of these
break down, don't hesitate to let me know and I'll come over.'

The city man was surprised and delighted. 'How nice! Thank
you! So do you fix things?' 'No,' replied the plain man. 'I have no
idea how to fix these things. But I will be happy to show you how
to live without them.'

How Does Your Garden Grow?

GROWING PAINS PART 2
*

There's a production line set up in the greenhouse. Seed trays and little pots at one end of the potting bench. On the ground a tub of compost and a bag of vermiculite (something that is new to me, but it increases water and nutrient retention and aerates the soil, I'm reliably informed). Next to the pots is an old biscuit tin holding the packets of seeds that have been arriving in the post periodically for the last week or so, and at the far end a box of wooden plant labels that look like lollipop sticks. I can see Emma through the glass, bundled up in multiple layers against the cold, hat pulled down almost to her nose, methodically filling trays and pots with compost, sprinkling vermiculite, counting out seeds.

I'm weeding. The raised beds are done, and stand bare-earthed and expectant. The gravel between them has also been relieved of a forest of weeds that the winter hadn't quite managed to kill off. 'Winter doesn't kill weeds,' Emma says, when I complain to her that they are still very much alive. 'It's a common misconception. Weeds are like any other plant. Some are annuals and just die off once they've seeded, and others are perennials and die back only to return, full of vim and vigour, in the spring.'

'Shit,' I say.

She shrugs. 'Sorry.'

This winter anyway has, so far, been mild, wet and frost-free. It is only now, in February, that we are starting to get the weather that seems right for this time of year. This morning there was ice on the water troughs and the pipes to the outside taps were frozen. I had to carry buckets of water for the animals from the house. The forecast for the coming week predicts it will stay cold. It's a relief. It feels like the full stop that the plants and animals living in our temperate climate need to quietly gather their strength before the rigours of spring. It is the natural order of things.

I'm now tackling the long bed that runs alongside the greenhouse, where there will be a mixture of herbs and flowers and the perfect globe artichokes that I can already see in my mind's eye. Emma took pity on me doing battle with an ancient trowel and has lent me her special weeding tool. It is unlike any garden tool I have ever seen. The cylindrical handle is copper swaged onto a narrow, stainless steel blade that scoops up at the sides and is gently pointed at its tip. It is sleek, spare and perfectly designed for its purpose.

'Some bloke in his shed came up with the design,' Emma told me, 'and it's made by people who repair aeroplanes. It's called Uncle Peter's Garden Trowel.'

This sounds so staggeringly unlikely that I have to establish for myself if this is actually the case or just some whimsical fancy she has made up. And it turns out she hasn't. Who Uncle Peter is, or was, is unclear, but he was the original creator of this tool over 30 years ago. And it is indeed made by a company in Gloucestershire that does repairs and maintenance on light aircraft and gliders. They call it a 'generation trowel', fully expecting it to last long enough to be handed down to the next generation when they discover the joys of weeding. And it's guaranteed for life, which means it is unlikely ever to break and provide the perfect excuse to stop weeding. It is what Richard Sennett describes in his book *The Craftsman* as 'sublime'. For Sennett, the tool that deserves this moniker is the flat-edged screwdriver. He almost swoons as he writes:

> *Without hesitation, the flat-edged screwdriver can be described as sublime – the word sublime standing, as it does in philosophy and the arts, for the potently strange. In craftwork, that sentiment focuses especially on objects very simple in form that seemingly can do anything.*

I suspect if he had come across Uncle Peter's garden tool, he might have said much the same. Because it works, brilliantly, particularly on the deep-rooted dandelions and docks and the creeping buttercup, which I am developing a dangerously psychotic response to. 'Bloody stuff's everywhere,' I mutter as I ease out another clump of it. I've learned now not to just grab on to it and yank (which of course would be the most satisfying way of clearing it), because all that happens is that I end up with a handful of leaves, and the roots, which creep their way perniciously through the soil forming an intractable tangle, are left behind to reshoot almost in the time it takes to go and make a cup of tea and return.

It is satisfying though, this hands-on, grubby, manual labour, because the results are instantly apparent. An hour of enduring an achy back and stiff knees is rewarded, when I stand up to stretch everything out, by the clear evidence of what my labours have achieved. A freshly weeded bed is a thing of beauty and, more satisfying still is carrying the tub I've filled with the vanquished enemy and tipping it on to the bonfire pile.

By the time it is getting too dark to see, the vegetable garden is weed free and the greenhouse full of – according to Emma – 'at least a million' little pots and seed trays, all labelled and neatly arranged on the staging.

'Is that everything?' I ask.

'Lord, no! This is just the start. I've done most of the flowers. Next week we'll do the tomatoes, aubergines and artichokes. Oh, and I'll show you a trick with sweet peas, but can you gather together every loo roll you can find?'

'There's not much room left,' I observe.

'No, we'll need to get some more staging to stick over the other side and at the end, and we are also going to need a greenhouse heater just to keep the temperature above freezing otherwise nothing will germinate and I'll have filled a million pots for nothing.'

My job now, she tells me sternly, is to keep everything watered. 'And I got you some of these, which will make you love me even more.' Emma hands me a little bag containing three small plastic widgets. They screw on to the top of old plastic bottles, she explains, and work exactly like the rose on a watering can. If you water little pots and shallow seed trays with a normal watering can, it lets out too much water and the soil and the precious seeds can get washed away. These simple little attachments let out water at a perfect, gentle trickle.

'Genius!' I say.

And she gives me a nod of assent and drives off.

Over the next few weeks the greenhouse, which was already pretty full, is crammed with more and more trays and pots, crowded onto the extra staging I had bought, leaving only the narrowest strip of space to stand and work in. There are seeds that could be planted straight into the ground a little later in the year, but, said Emma, 'why wait for results when we can give them an early start?' So there are more trays of Cosmos. ('What were we thinking?' Emma asked with bemusement, when we realized how many Cosmos we'd actually planted. And cornflowers. Trays of them. Our plan was to share the plants between our respective gardens, but, observed Emma, 'if everything germinates and grows, we could supply every garden in south Wales'.)

My head had been turned by a photograph of lime-green tobacco plants in one of the pile of catalogues I was beginning to amass. Lime-green zinnia, too, both of which I thought would look incredibly striking amongst the jewel-like richness of the dahlias that I had ordered. So we had sown a packet each of them, as well as several gladioli bulbs, which Emma planted right at the bottom of large pots with a good 25 centimetres of earth above them. 'They'll never see the light of day, will they?' I ask. But that is what they like, apparently. And then there's the sweet peas. As instructed, I have collected every empty cardboard loo roll I can find and I am now filling them with potting compost and poking a single sweet pea seed down into each one. 'They like a narrow, deep root run,' Emma tells me. 'So loo rolls are just the job for starting them off.' The carrots, cucumbers, chillies, peppers, strawberries, beetroot, peas and beans have all been sown too, and there is now a special greenhouse heater rigged up and wafting warm air about, to keep them all frost free. I start researching preserving methods like drying and bottling, in anticipation of a bumper crop.

Simple Pleasure #6

— A BOX OF MANGOES —

———

I know. I'm aware that extolling the simple virtues of a box of exotic fruit that has been flown halfway across the world is stretching the concept of simplicity possibly beyond its limits. And it seems particularly daft when I'm spending all this time trying to grow fruit and vegetables in my own garden. But I'm going to, because these mangoes are worth taking some flak for. And with the best will in the world, they won't grow in Wales.

Our neighbours, Mark and Jo, who live down the hill from us, are having a midsummer party. They moved in last autumn and this is a sort of housewarming as well as a general celebration of their first summer in the Wye Valley. It hasn't been much of a summer so far, so it is a brave plan to hold a lunchtime picnic in the garden for over a hundred guests. Some of the people invited are coming from further afield, and as the lunchtime picnic is expected to run until it's time for evening drinks and well beyond, it will be far too late (and probably not legal) for them to try and get home. So, we have offered beds within staggering distance, although it is quite a steep stagger.

Martin and Katrin, who stayed with Mark and Jo earlier in the year and who we met over supper, take us up on the offer. They arrive on Friday night, slightly harassed after frustrating hours in the car sitting in weekend traffic. But the rain that has been falling unremittingly since the beginning of the week has now stopped. It is one of those beautiful rare evenings, warm, almost sultry, the light golden, the air full of the scent of roses. And it's late June and light until almost 10pm. We sit outside with glasses of chilled pink wine, a simple supper of roast chicken and salad, catching up on life's events since we last saw each other.

The following morning I get up early, go through the usual routine of checking and feeding animals, letting out the hens and ducks and collecting the eggs. It is already promising to be a beautiful day – hot too – which will be a huge relief for our hosts. I take the dogs on a walk through the fields and woods around the house, dropping down to the ponds in the valley so they can swim before we head home.

Martin and Katrin are up and sitting outside with mugs of coffee when we get back. *Perfect guests*, I think. I love it when the people who come to stay are self-sufficient, will happily find their way around the kitchen and help themselves. On the table beside them is a cardboard box, flat, rectangular and quite large. 'To thank you for having us to stay.' I lift off the top and inside, nestled in shredded paper, are rows of beautiful mangoes. Their skins are deep yellow, blushed with orange, their shape as smooth and curvaceous as a Hepworth sculpture. And when I pick one up, press lightly with my fingers, I feel the flesh softly yielding. They are perfect.

'It is mango season in India,' Martin explains, 'and at this time of year all the Indian-owned shops around us, even the butchers and the hardware shop, sell boxes of mangoes. It is almost like a festival – there's this wonderful anticipation of them arriving, people talk about it for days. The season is short – by the end of the month it will be over – so everyone goes a bit mango mad.'

'Let's have some for breakfast!' And I gently peel away the thin skins to reveal the even more-intensely yellow-orange fruit beneath and release the sweetly perfumed fragrance. These are Alphonso mangoes and not for nothing have they earned the reputation as the king of mangoes. I gently slice the slippery flesh away from the flat stone in the middle and put it in a bowl. The mother of a family I stayed with when I first went to Africa would serve mangoes with a squeeze of lime juice. It was a heavenly combination: the clean, sharpness of the lime seemed to enhance the sweetness of the mango. So I do the same now, zesting a lime and sprinkling the orange fruit with flecks of zingy green. And then I squeeze the juice over and together we eat the gloriously messy slices with our fingers – to use a spoon would be to miss the point, because eating a mango like this has to involve all the senses, and licking the juice from around your chin and off your fingers is part of the deep, deep pleasure they bring.

*

Building
a Future

EXPEDITION EARTHSHIP
*

Paul and I are sitting in the kitchen having lunch after a busy morning in the garden. Paul is a tree-surgeon and has come to take down a couple of damaged branches from a tree overhanging the pig pen, and I, as ever, have been weeding – cursing, and at the same time feeling grudging admiration for, creeping buttercup. It has an unerring habit of putting down its deep, intractable roots amongst other plants that it seems to know I want to keep. It hides, lurking beneath the leaves of the geraniums, which look very similar to its own leaves, perfectly camouflaged. I stand to admire the bed that I've spent a morning clearing, enjoying the newly exposed rich, brown soil between the foliage and flowers of the herbs and shrubs. I walk away, satisfied the job is done, and as soon as my back is turned, out the buttercup creeps...

Our conversation is about houses. Paul and his wife Sian recently bought their first house and he's telling me their plans for it. We start imagining what our perfect houses would be if we could build them, and what elements they would need to incorporate to meet our respective ideas of perfection. For the last few years I have been quietly imagining the house I'd like to build one day. The house that will see us out. I have a floorplan in my head that I mentally play around with, but the essential elements remain the same. It is a house that has everything I think we need and nothing more. A single living space to cook, eat and sit. A room that is the buffer between outside and in – the muddy space for coats and boots. (We have one now and I don't mind admitting it is my favourite room in the house.) Somewhere to sleep, a place to wash. Outside there will be vegetable beds. And my luxury – a pond big enough to swim in.

But my greatest wish – and one that I won't compromise on – is that the house works in tune with the earth. That it is built with materials that are natural, in a way that allows it to function without the need for finite and damaging resources. And this is not just for the long-term sake of the environment, but also for the pragmatic sake of our finances. To put it bluntly, I don't want to reach a stage when I am scrabbling under the cushions on the sofa in the hope of finding enough stray coins to pay the heating bill.

'You should build an Earthship,' says Paul, matter-of-factly.

'An Earthship?' I repeat, questioningly, in a slightly disparaging tone.

I met Paul soon after we moved to Wales. Young, energetic, curious about everything, he is one of life's great enthusiasts. Formal education was wasted on him. He is dyslexic, but is also someone who was never going to be stimulated by being shut indoors, gazing at a blackboard. The countryside has been his classroom. His extensive knowledge of trees and wildlife is all self-taught. He has excellent bushcraft skills too, but it is his hunger always to learn more that I love about him most.

'Have you been watching one of those bonkers American TV programmes about UFOs again?'

'They're houses,' Paul tells me, through mouthfuls of sandwich. 'They're amazing – all off-grid and built of tyres and bottles.'

So I look them up. I start to read about them and Michael Reynolds, the rogue architect who came up with the concept of using rubbish as building materials to create homes that had no need for utilities. It was the late 60s, the hippy era. New Mexico, where Reynolds had based himself, was a place that drew in hippies from all over the United States and the world in search of Utopia amongst its wild, untamed landscapes. Building houses that harnessed the earth's resources may have started as the whim of an idealistic hippy, but half a century later they are still being built. And it appeared from my research that Michael Reynolds himself is still building them. There's an Earthship community, north of a place called Taos, where there's a visitor centre and the office of Earthship Biotecture. And they have an intern programme. People of any age, with no building experience, can sign up and go and help build one.

By now my brain is racing. Just the idea of heading out to New Mexico for little less than a month is exciting and terrifying in equal measure. Surely, I think, I'd be by far the oldest person there. Would I be physically up to it? And I have no idea how to build anything. I'm cack-handed with a drill, never seem to be able to take accurate measurements, hang pictures at jaunty angles, convinced they are straight. I can do grunt work: split wood, muck out barns, shovel earth. But I have no skills. I can't do anything useful or practical.

But still the idea niggles away. I was thinking back to what Satish Kumar had said: 'Our hands are made to make...' So I send an email to the Earthship office. A day later, I get a reply from a woman called Lauren. We talk on the phone. She confirms there are spaces left on the intern programme at the end of the year, that my age isn't an issue – 'Michael is 74 and he's still on site every day,' she tells me – and that if I want to come she'll email me the registration form. 'Do it!' my brain shouts. 'Sign me up,' I say to Lauren, before I can come up with a reason not to go. 'See you at the end of the year.'

HOT DOG, JUMPING FROG...
*

... Albuquerque. I'm humming the Prefab Sprout song as I walk off the plane and through the airport. I collect my bag, laden with wellies, thermals, waterproof trousers, working gloves, safety glasses and a tool belt. My fellow passengers had been discussing the big snowstorm that had hit Albuquerque the day before. It's dark when I trundle out of the airport building looking for the bus to the rental car place. Early evening (although well into the middle of the night as far as my body clock is concerned). There doesn't seem to be much in the way of snow – a few remnants on verges – but it's very cold. My nose tingles and starts to run. A large, convivial woman in outsize furry earmuffs (leopard print) shows me to my car after I've dealt with the paperwork.

It's quite a drive to get out to the Earthship HQ – three hours or so – so I've booked into an airport motel for the night. I fall into a grateful sleep, only to be wide awake three hours later: the time I would be getting up at home. I read a bit. Have a shower. Read, snooze, re-pack in a slightly aimless, time-wasting fashion, snooze a bit more until finally the dark sky lightens to grey and I get up and sling my bag back into the car.

The motel breakfast is one of those impossibly gloomy, everything-out-of-a-packet affairs. I wander around the edge of the room trying not to think of the amount of plastic that must get used and thrown away in the thousands of motels like this right across the country. All the cutlery, plates, bowls and cups are disposable. There are pre-made omelettes that are delivered by the sack, as are the 'roasted' squares of potato. Sachets of sauce, small plastic tubs of jam and margarine. The only non-processed things are the apples, which have been individually wrapped in acres of cling film. I toast a piece of raisin bread, swill back a cup of coffee and leave. Or try to leave, but the windscreen and all the windows of the car are opaque with a thick layer of ice. Impatiently I scrape at it with my driver's licence, the car's heater doing little to help, until there's enough clear glass to see through. I'm on my way!

I point the car north on the freeway. It's a weekend and there is not much traffic at this hour. On either side of the road the land is flat; a dusty, olive-green expanse of scrubby sagebrush, with occasional startlingly white patches of snow. It is interspersed by the ubiquitous, low-rise strip malls of American roadways. Fast food. Used cars. Each one as featureless and unmemorable as the next. I'm trying to quell a sense of disappointment. I thought New Mexico would be different. Feel more like a remote outpost, a still wild west. But it's easy driving and steadily I eat up the miles, skirting around Santa Fe, joining a narrower highway and then turning off to pass through a gorge, running alongside a river.

Red, rocky outcrops rise up on either side of the road; the bare branches of cottonwood trees; small, twisted junipers. Ravens soar, deep dark silhouettes against the grey sky. There are wooden cabins and low adobe houses that seem to grow out of the earth. Battered pick-up trucks, wood piles, stockades. I lower the car windows, letting the cold, crisp air rush in. It's high here. Albuquerque is just over 1,600 metres above sea level. I've gained another 500 metres since then. There's more snow too. *This is more like it!* I think, and can feel myself grinning.

As I reach the edge of Taos I follow signs to the Plaza. The side roads are white with hard-packed snow and even the main road that seems to run through this small town is snow-covered and slushy. There is little in the way of traffic or people, even though it is late morning by now.

I find a place to park, dig wellies out of my bag, pull on a bobble hat and go in search of proper coffee.

I've travelled to various bits of America over the years – both coasts, through the middle, parts of the south and right up to the northernmost community in Alaska. But I don't remember ever being in a town quite like Taos. I'm not even sure it would count as a town. It is more village in size, compact, with narrow streets, pavements and small independent shops, cafes and bars. If you can tell anything about a population from its local town, then the people who live in and around Taos like cooking, books, outdoor gear, coffee, dogs and art. Since the latter part of the 19th century, artists began to settle in Taos and the Taos Society of Artists was formed in 1915. The art scene – if the number of galleries is anything to go by (apparently there are more than 80) – is still very much alive.

I find a café, its windows steamed up, and I gratefully enter its warm fug. The atmosphere is friendly, genuinely hospitable; not the empty, insincere version of hospitality that has become so widespread, particularly in places frequented by tourists. I order coffee and eggs and flick through the local magazine that I had picked up in the Plaza. The opening article explains what makes Taos different, and its assessment seemed, even in the very short time I had been there, to be entirely true. 'We have more galleries than gas stations, more museums and historic homes than grocery stores. Heck, many of our roads don't even have streetlamps.' And it is also a place where people say hello on the street and have conversations in shops. 'Like home,' I smile to myself, as I leave Mudd N Flood (I can never resist looking around a shop selling outdoor gear – even if I don't want to buy anything), with an invitation from Tam, who was working there, to come back and meet Chris and

Elana, the owners. 'They can tell you so much about the area,' she said, 'and I think you'll find lots of common ground.'

But now I can't hang around. I have to find one of the rare grocery stores, pick up some food and get to the Earthship HQ because I have to check in. The intern programme doesn't start until Monday, but Lauren has kindly arranged for me to spend a night in one of the Earthships so that I can test out whether a house with no heating, no mains electricity or mains water, built out of tyres, aluminium cans and glass bottles, would be bearable to live in, even if the temperature outside is well below freezing. Which it is.

A NIGHT IN AN EARTHSHIP
*

I leave Taos behind, drive out on a road that cuts through the mesa – a wide treeless expanse of sagebrush with dramatic, rugged snow-capped mountains on the Eastern horizon. I cross the Rio Grande, pull over to gaze down the gorge the river has carved through the red-brown earth, then drive on a short distance until I see a strange building: a building like I've never seen before. It is tall, a Gaudi-esque, fairy-tale structure of columns and arches, huge windows with elaborate metalwork frames, the walls studded with thousands of cans and bottles forming intricate patterns reminiscent of tribal art.

I turn off the road at the sign for the visitor centre. This building is very different. Low rise, windows running its length, crowded with plants. I walk into a room that is not dissimilar from any visitor centre. There's a welcome desk, literature, T-shirts for sale. And it's warm, almost tropical-feeling in contrast to the cold, dry air outside. I take off my coat and walk with it slung over my arm while I follow the short self-guided tour around the building.

The span of windows I had seen from the outside forms the wall of a corridor that links the various rooms. South facing, it doubles as a greenhouse. There are tomatoes, Physalis, fig trees and banana trees, growing in the depths of winter at over 2,000 metres. It is the heat generated by the floor to ceiling, south-facing windows of the greenhouse that warms the whole structure, and in theory that heat doesn't escape, because the other outer walls of the building are constructed of old tyres, packed tight with earth, laid like giant circular bricks and covered in more earth, creating a super-insulated heat store.

Rainwater is collected, stored, used and re-used, thanks to a clever system of filters and ingenious plumbing. Electricity is generated by solar panels and a small windmill.

Beyond the visitor centre, spread out over 600 acres of the mesa, is the Greater Earthship Community. There are plots of land for sale. The plots are circular and range from half an acre to three. There are sites for a total of 130 homes and plots are not allowed to be fenced, so the elk, coyote and other animals that live out here can move around freely. So this is low-density housing.

Adam, who I follow down the dirt road to the house I'm staying in, tells me there are 79 fully functioning homes here and 7 more under construction. But as I look out through the windscreen, it is hard to pick out more than a few homes, and even those sit so discreetly within the landscape, they are barely visible.

We turn into a gateway beside a low, rounded, snow-covered hump, which is actually the back of the house. We park outside large, double wooden doors and walk through an arch in an adobe wall, the colour of burnished copper, to a door. The door is set in a wall made of glass bottles laid in concrete, creating an effect like stained glass. Beyond the door is a huge room – 'the garage', Adam tells me. It is so beautiful, it seems wrong to drive a muddy car into it. The south-facing span of the greenhouse begins here too. There are plants and even a fish pond. Another door brings us into the main body of the house. The greenhouse corridor is filled with bougainvillea, rosemary, scented geraniums, a huge fig tree, tomatoes.

'Help yourself to anything you want to eat,' says Adam, as he leads me into the first room off the greenhouse. I gasp. It is not at all what I expected. It is, well, opulent – a large open-plan room with sofas and a huge TV at one end, a dining-room table and chairs in the middle and a kitchen with a large fridge and a gas range. 'There's Netflix and all that stuff,' Adam tells me, waving at the telly, 'and Wi-Fi – the code is in the book. Everything works here like a normal kitchen, you just have to turn the oven on when you want to use it, otherwise it just wastes power. But it uses propane gas for cooking – it's the one thing we can't generate enough solar power to do. The water in the little tap beside the main one is for drinking.'

'I didn't expect it to be so...' I struggle to find the word.

'Normal?' Adam laughs. 'That's what everyone says, but that's Mike's idea. He built this to prove you can live in an Earthship pretty much exactly the way you would live in a normal house. You don't have to make big compromises or sacrifices.'

There are two bedrooms, both with bathrooms, bottle walls, stained glass, beautiful tiles.

'It's more like an art installation than a house,' I say to myself. It's also incredibly warm but there are no radiators, no underfloor heating and no fireplace. I've shed layers of clothing and am now just in a T-shirt, yet just beyond the glass there is snow on the ground and the sun is low in the sky. Adam shows me how to open a vent to regulate the temperature. 'But shut it at night, otherwise all the plants will die and you'll get very cold. Enjoy your stay!'

After he leaves, I walk around the house again, admiring all the little details, the artistry of it, but also marvelling at its practicality. I bundle up in coat and hat to look at it once more from the outside. It is so low profile and unobtrusive, as are the other buildings that I can just make out in the distance. The sun is casting an orange-pink glow on the snow-covered mountains. The air is still, the silence deep. I stand, almost in a trance, until the cold drives me back into the warm embrace of this extraordinary building.

I make tea. I read. Watch an episode of *The Crown*. The sky turns deep indigo, then black. There is no light pollution, the darkness is deep and infinite. Stars appear above the greenhouse roof. I shut the vents and go and cook supper. The shower is hot, the loo flushes. The thick adobe walls of the bedroom make it feel like a cocoon. I snuggle down into bed, read some more, then switch off the light and fall into a contented sleep.

THE CAN HOUSE AND OTHER STORIES
*

Over breakfast the next morning I read one of the books that have been left out on the coffee table. It is called *Journey* and it is Mike Reynolds's account of how the Earthships came into being – their evolution. He was born in 1945 in Kentucky and went to study architecture at the University of Cincinnati. His ideas were viewed as radical even in the early days. His concept for an urban residential housing scheme was published in an architectural journal in 1969 and was equally condemned and praised. 'This', he writes, 'has been the pattern of my working life ever since. It caused me to take neither seriously.'

It also made him realize that he did not ever want to practise 'standard' architecture, that he wanted to do things differently. And he made the headlines in 1970, soon after a news report he watched on the television, which talked about the number of beer and soda cans littering the countryside and its prediction that the problem of rubbish would only get worse. The same news programme also included a story on clearcutting timber for housing, and raised concerns on the environmental damage this practice might cause, as well as the likelihood of a rise in timber prices, and therefore the cost of housing. Mike built a house out of beer cans. It cost $11,000 and still stands today, but although it garnered him a lot of publicity, it was seen as a novelty – a bit of a joke – rather than a serious response to a serious social issue.

By then Mike had moved out to Taos County, but although he wanted to live differently and to keep trying out the ideas that crowded his head, he didn't see himself as part of the hippy set. In fact, he came to New Mexico to ride motocross bikes, hoping to get injured and avoid being called up to go to Vietnam. He bought some land with an old barn on it and it was there that he started using anything he could find as materials to do what he needed to do. He came up with a way of using bottles as bricks and built his first house out of tyres. New Mexico back then was rather lax as far as building permits were concerned and this was crucial, as it allowed for experimentation. 'Today's world simply does not allow for learning,' he writes, 'thus we are not evolving fast enough to survive.'

Mike started experimenting with solar gain and holding on to that naturally generated warmth using the mass of earth-stuffed tyres as a heat store. His aim was to create houses that looked like extensions of the earth itself – 'we can extend the earth, but we can't replace it.' But his ideas and his dogmatic approach proved too extreme for many of those around him. Wives came and went, people came to work with him, but often left soon afterwards. 'I was trying to make it easy for people to move in the direction I was thinking, but it was too radical, too lonely and too hard. I learned to soften my thinking as I introduced it to the public. It only took me about 20 years to learn this...'

The Turbine House was the turning point. Known as the 'Grandaddy of Earthships', it was the first building Mike designed and built that really addressed what he had identified as the key elements of survival, without caring what the building looked like. It heated and cooled itself, provided its own power from wind and sun, contained and treated its own sewage and created a space and climate to grow food. In 1980 he moved in. He had no mortgage, no debts, no utility bills and that is when he started to think: *what if this was available for everyone?*

Over the following years Mike continued to experiment, to hone his ideas. Volkshouses were an attempt to find a solar design that could be repeated, possibly even mass-produced. The Pit houses he built next were the final step that led to what today he calls Earthships. He built the first one in 1988 – a series of U-shaped rooms facing south and connected by a greenhouse hallway. It proved to be the easiest to build and best performing of all his previous buildings and he still lives in it today.

Adam drops by to feed the fish in the garage fish pond. I have to pack up – new guests are arriving. I could have stayed on site – interns can stay very cheaply in dormitory-style accommodation in some of the older Earthships that belong to the company – but I knew I'd want my own space. I'd found a cabin on a farm not far away and will check in later.

In the meantime, I ask Adam if I am allowed to walk through the Earthship community if I stick to the access road, just to get a bit more of a feel for it.

'Sure,' he says. 'Just don't knock on any doors or look through windows. I'm going up to the Phoenix at 11. You can drop in and see it if you want to.'

The access road is a simple dirt track, just wide enough for two cars, that winds through the sagebrush. It had been another cold night – not that I had noticed – and the mud beneath my feet is frozen into solid ruts and runnels. But the sun is bright in a clear blue sky, the outline of the mountains sharp, the sagebrush giving off its herby, earthy scent. I walk past an unfinished house and wonder if it might be one that I will work on during my time here. Like the house I had stayed in, it is beautiful – if anything, even more elaborate. Bottles are carefully stacked outside, separated by colour. From what I can see from the road, the interior bottle and can walls are as intricate and painstakingly assembled as mosaics. I wonder, as I walk, how long these buildings take to complete.

The mesa looks flat, but it is deceptive. It dips and rises. There are dry water courses, rocky outcrops. There are footprints in the snow – rabbits and those of a dog or maybe a coyote. A car drives past; the driver waves. Every now and then another building comes into view, rising out of the vegetation. They all differ slightly. These are not mass-produced houses of one design. Some are smaller, simpler. Some look almost like castles.

It takes me about half an hour to reach the Phoenix, which is at the far end of the community's land. I had seen pictures of it – it is another of the company's Earthships that is rented out and, like all of the rental properties, it is also for sale. Adam is cleaning it in preparation for the day's guests.

'Come and have a look,' he says. 'It's kinda crazy.'

'Wow,' I breathe, as I step into the greenhouse. This is not a corridor but a cavernous glass room, full of plants and ponds. There are fish and terrapins. Parakeets. Huge trees and shrubs. It is as fecund and humid as a rainforest. In common with the other Earthships, the main living spaces are reached from a door in the greenhouse, but at the Phoenix the greenhouse continues inside. There are beds of plants meandering between the kitchen and sitting area, trees reaching up to the ceiling. Amongst this verdant maze there are cave-like bedrooms, tunnels, underground rooms, bathrooms with bottle walls and hand-made bathtubs sculpted in adobe. A fireplace dominates the sitting room, a huge stone and adobe affair, the adobe dyed green, studded with mosaic and edged with fairy lights. The fire is gas, and at the flick of a switch a curtain of water falls in front of it.

'Kinda crazy' is one way to describe it. I feel a sort of sensory overload, as if I'm hallucinating. It is too much; exhausting, actually. But for all its eccentricities and whimsy it still works as an Earthship should. I find out later that Mike built it in response to someone who had commissioned an Earthship to be built for him, but wanted to alter the design. His ideas and the alterations he wanted to incorporate would have compromised the building's functionality in Mike's opinion, so Mike refused to build it. His client was furious. He never got his Earthship, but Mike still went ahead and built the Phoenix, just to prove his point. It's for sale now – yours for $1.5 million.

LEARNING BY DOING
*

On Monday morning I return to the Earthship HQ to meet my fellow interns and find out what the plans are for the week. There are around 16 of us; one young man from Canada, the rest from various parts of the US. Ages range from early twenties to early fifties (there is one person older than me!) and there are two or three more women than men. Some are trainee or practising architects, there are a few working as wilderness guides and park rangers, and there's also an archaeologist and a photographer. They all express an interest and a wish to one day build their own homes and all were drawn here by the environmental merits of the Earthships. There are three homes that are currently being worked on, so we will be split into three groups and each assigned a building project. There will be the option of moving around to the other sites in the following weeks, to get hands-on experience of different aspects of the construction.

The rest of the day is free to allow everyone to settle in, get their bearings, buy food. I'd checked into my cabin the day before and already feel very at home. It is on a small farm, nestled in a canyon, with a great wall of mountains at the back and far-reaching views down the valley to the green-blue expanse where the mesa meets the sky. The farm belongs to Eric and Elizabeth, who I met that afternoon, bundled up against the cold, walking their two dachshunds in the snow. Eric is tall and thin, grey hair in a ponytail (there are a lot of ponytails in this neck of the woods), with a kind, laid-back demeanour. Elizabeth is Swedish and a beauty, a thick bob of blonde hair poking out beneath her sheepskin hat, cheekbones you could sharpen a knife on. They farm goji berries, fruit and vegetables on a small scale, although the fields lie dormant and snow-covered now. They also have chickens and turkeys, a couple of sheep and alpacas and a donkey.

'A menagerie!' I say. 'I have one too!'

They live in an old log cabin and there are various other small cabins dotted around the farm.

'They were here when we bought the place,' Eric tells me. 'We didn't have to do anything other than a bit of renovation.'

The farm and its older buildings – the main log house and some of the cabins – date back to the early 20th century and have quite a history. At that time, Taos and this area of New Mexico had become a centre for the arts. At the invitation of the wealthy society hostess and arts patron Mabel Dodge Luhan, D H Lawrence and his wife Frieda visited in 1922. Luhan's house in Taos hosted many of the artistic luminaries of the time – Georgia O'Keeffe, Ansel Adams – but she was a notoriously difficult person – described by a biographer as 'a woman of profound contradictions. She was generous. She was petty. Domineering and endearing'. And the Lawrences finally fell out with her, so went to stay at a guest house belonging to her husband and then later at another belonging to friends: a cabin on this farm. They left Taos for Mexico in 1923, but returned the following year, again to stay with Luhan. And once more there was a clash of personalities. So Luhan, wanting to keep them in Taos, gave them a ranch. (Can you imagine?!) Lawrence tried to refuse, but Frieda accepted it, saying they could give Luhan the manuscript of *Sons and Lovers* in return.

The ranch – now called, unsurprisingly, D H Lawrence Ranch – is just up the hill from here. Lawrence wrote much of his novel *St Mawr* there, and began *The Plumed Serpent*. They left New Mexico in 1925, with plans to return, but never did. By then he had been diagnosed with TB and so went back to Europe. He died in France in 1930, but at Frieda's request his remains were exhumed and cremated and his ashes brought back to the ranch to be buried there.

Aldous Huxley, who visited Lawrence while he was living here, returned in 1937. He lived in one of the cabins here and built an outhouse that still stands today. It was here that he wrote his collection of essays *Ends and Means*. When Eric and Elizabeth bought the place a decade ago, they found watercolours and letters by D H Lawrence in the attic.

I wonder if the attraction of being here for Lawrence and Huxley was the simplicity? Perhaps living in wooden cabins, surrounded by trees and mountains, immersed in nature, was a source of inspiration? The cabin I'm staying in is part of a long, single-storey adobe building. It has one main room – a bed-sitting room – with a woodburning stove and windows on both sides that flood the white interior with light. There's a small kitchen just off it and a bathroom. Eric shows me a route I can walk around the farm, and another trail that leads up to the back of the canyon. It is simple, but I have everything I need.

Our group is put to work on a building that is being overseen by Mike himself. The snow has melted, leaving a claggy sea of mud around the house, so we leave our cars and walk down to the site. There are a few people already there when we arrive, including a man we assume is Mike. He is small, with long grey hair and grey stubble. He wears a sheepskin hat pulled low over his forehead, black fleece, coat and jeans, snow boots. He has pale blue eyes, set close together. He pays us no regard whatsoever. In fact, there is no welcome, no introductions from anybody. A man – he doesn't give his name – tells us that concrete needs to be mixed, a wall needs plastering and bottles collected and prepared for a bottle wall. Brittany, the photographer, and I volunteer to work with bottles. 'You go with Nick,' we are told, and we follow a slightly taciturn-looking man out to his truck.

'We need to go out to the recycling bins by the office and collect bottles from there,' he says.

So we follow him there and start sorting through the boxes and bins.

'Any particular bottles that we should go for?' Brittany asks.

'Clear ones are good, those are the ones we use most of,' Nick says. 'Not brown. Green are OK, and pick up any blue ones. There was supposed to be a bottle delivery today but it hasn't come. So we'll just have to take what we can find here.'

Beneath the ice and snow Brittany and I find and gather up a good selection of bottles, load them into the back of Nick's truck and return to the site. The bottles will be turned into bricks, which will be used to build one of the interior walls of the house. This is done by cutting them in half, discarding the top half and washing the bottom half. The bottom halves are then matched up with another half of a similar diameter and taped together to form a 'bottle brick'. These are then laid, flat ends facing outwards, in a bed of concrete, and built up meticulously to form the intricately patterned glass walls that are synonymous with Earthships.

But there's a problem with the cutting machine, which is missing some crucial bit. And there are not enough buckets. Nick will sort it after lunch, he tells us, 'which is kinda now'. And he, Mike and all the other workers get in their trucks and drive away, leaving us interns to find somewhere to perch out of the mud and eat the lunches we have brought with us. No one says much about their morning. We talk about other things. But I suspect we are all hoping that we will feel a bit more useful and a bit less in the way as time goes on. After half an hour we are all expecting to get back to work, but it's over an hour before Mike and his team return.

That afternoon, when the bottle saw is finally fixed and Nick shows us how the bottles are to be cut, Brittany and I set up a pretty efficient production line, sorting, cutting and washing bottles. We confess to each other that the day hasn't been quite as we imagined; that we've felt a bit spare and useless. 'Maybe it'll get better,' I say with an optimism I don't really feel. 'It's the first day...'

I drive back to my cabin with mixed emotions. Has it been a mistake to come here? I can't work it out. The concept of Earthships, what Mike has achieved and what he is doing now, is as fascinating and inspiring as I hoped, but I am wondering how much I will actually learn being here, if every day is like today. I need a walk to help order my thoughts, but the sun has already set and I'm not yet familiar enough with my surroundings to venture out into the dark with a head torch, as I would at home.

Instead I light a fire, read, cook some supper, distract myself with menial but pleasing tasks like washing up. I have a book – it's here with me – called (rather marvellously) *Washing Up is Good for You*. It is a collection of essays that extol the virtues of small domestic tasks – cleaning a bathroom, cooking, repairing something, even making a cup of tea – and how, done with awareness, with mindfulness, they can reduce feelings of stress, make you feel calmer, give your mind space to think. Meredith Whitely, food writer and meditation teacher, says on the subject of washing up: 'there is a beauty and joy in finishing a small task – if we allow ourselves the time to recognize it'. It's true. After a day where I felt I had achieved nothing at all, a day that felt like a battle, to be able to do a task without asking how to do it or where the tools are that I need to complete it, and to be able to stand back and enjoy the results, was – well – comforting.

The next morning I get up and head out as the sky starts to lighten. I walk. It's not a long walk. It doesn't involve much in the way of navigation, even though I've never done it before. There are no hills to climb. But there are unfamiliar views and smells. Birds and plants I don't recognize. There is no traffic and no one else in the valley is out yet. This silent world of frost and ice is, for the moment, all mine. And in this oasis of calm I decide, as my boots crunch over the frozen earth, that I haven't made a mistake coming here; that whatever transpires over the next three weeks it will still be valuable, that I will still learn and discover things. So when I arrive on site and the bottle delivery still hasn't turned up, I go and introduce myself to one of the other members of the Earthship team, ask if there is something I can do to help him.

'Sure,' says Jim. 'We need to get all the interior walls plastered with concrete before we can start covering them with adobe. Two of the interns are doing the main room, but you can help me in here.' I have never plastered anything in my life. Never held the tools that I discover are called a hawk and a trowel. I load up a bucket with concrete, heave it to the foot of the wall Jim wants me to start on, load up the grey, rubbly porridge-like mixture onto my hawk and, using the trowel, attempt to imitate Jim's graceful scoop and sweep manoeuvre, which leaves a smooth, broad smear of concrete on the wall, like buttercream on a cake. It's not a success. A large glob of concrete falls to the floor with the sound of a cowpat. 'Shit,' I mutter. Jim says nothing. There's no reproach, no rolling eyes. He just carries on. And so do I.

By the end of the day both my shoulders are aching. I'm filthy, I've got concrete in my hair, but there is also plenty of concrete where it should be – on the wall. It's not very smooth, but Jim says that doesn't matter – the adobe will cover it. I feel ridiculously pleased with myself, return to my cabin elated and exhausted to the glorious luxury of a hot shower. I finish the wall the next day, with Brittany's help (she too has given up on the bottles).

'Adobe tomorrow,' says Jim.

Mike wants all the walls that have been concreted to get a coat of adobe today, so five of us set about erecting scaffolding, while Jim and Dale, another intern who has proved to be adept at mixing concrete, make the first batch of adobe. Adobe is a mix of sand, finely sifted earth, chopped straw and water. It is one of the oldest building materials in the world and many of the older buildings in New Mexico – as well as modern ones – are built from adobe bricks.

Just outside Taos is Taos Pueblo. A World Heritage Site, it has been home to the Native American tribe of Puebloans for around a thousand years and is still inhabited today. The village is built on either side of Red Willow Creek. There are low-rise adobe homes and shops built around a warren of narrow streets. Outside many of the buildings are domed ovens called *hornos*, also built of adobe. But the most startling structures are the two 'apartment' buildings. Each home within the blocks is owned by a family and passed down from one generation to the next. A home is typically two rooms and each one is self-contained – there are no passageways between the houses. The building on the north side of the creek is quite beautiful, its thick adobe walls are the red of the earth. Behind it are the majestic Taos mountains and the great grand arc of the sky. It is the largest building of its kind still standing and said to be one of the most photographed and painted buildings in North America. It deserves that title.

So the use of adobe in the building of the Earthships seems entirely fitting. It is this ancient, natural material that gives them their soft, organic shapes and allows them to sit so unobtrusively in the landscape. The inner and outer walls of this house will be coated with multiple layers of adobe, the final one being so fine the walls will be as smooth and even as painted clay. But they take time to dry – in the winter as much as a week – which is why Mike is keen to complete this first layer in just a day. It is a true team effort, but we all relish the physicality of it; hard, manual labour that also feels creative. With every sweep of our trowels we are moulding and shaping the walls of this building, putting flesh on its bones. As I lug a heavy bucket up on to the scaffolding for the umpteenth time (and get called 'buff' by one of my – much younger – fellow interns, which makes me laugh) I realize that I'm loving this. It feels useful. I feel useful. And very content.

PERHAPS I'M NOT CUT OUT FOR THIS AFTER ALL
*

Monday morning of the second week. Our little gang has been moved on to another project, a home that is nearing completion. It is much bigger, much more elaborate than the previous one, and has taken two years to reach the stage it is at now. The greenhouse is double width, making the whole structure feel lighter, airier and more opulent. The bottle walls have been built by Heather, the acknowledged 'bottle queen'. She's been working on Earthships for 18 years and the walls she has created for this house are the most intricate and complex I've seen. Even my frustratingly short experience of preparing bottle bricks, and laying a few, has given me enough insight to know the level of skill and the number of hours that have gone into the completion of these walls.

This Earthship is what is known as the Global model. Mike's wish to make Earthships acceptable and accessible to as many people as possible has led him to come up with three designs, although all of them can be customized to an extent. The Global model is the most expensive – working out at about $250 per square foot. The previous building we worked on was an Encounter. Smaller and a bit more basic, it is significantly cheaper to build. And then there is the Simple Survival, a domed studio room, with a greenhouse corridor and a bathroom.

Our foreman this week is Gunner. He takes us around the house and shows us the level of finish he expects. The adobe work is complete and the walls are smooth and cream and flawless. There are beautiful floors and cabinet work. It all seems way out of our league. There are tiles to lay in the kitchen, a door to build and some more basic, but still precise carpentry – which is what Dale and I get assigned to do. We look rather nervously at each other and confess, when we are out of Gunner's earshot, that neither of us is confident in the use of a drill, or table saws, nor do we think we have the mindset needed for meticulous measuring. We are tasked with measuring, cutting and sanding three planks of wood and fitting them inside a door frame. It doesn't sound exactly taxing, but oh, we make a meal of it.

'I think I should stick to mixing adobe,' says Dale, as he measures and remeasures to try and work out where to drill the holes for the screws.

'And I should stick to applying it,' I say, through gritted teeth, as I try to work out how to use a carpenter square, getting more and more frustrated at my own ineptness. Eventually, after a painfully long time and badgering Gunner with endless questions, we manage to get the three boards in place, but it doesn't feel like much of an achievement. Gone is that lovely sensation of being useful. Today, once again, I just feel in the way. The woodwork around the front door needs staining, which we feel a bit more able to tackle, but as the day comes to an end, I wonder what on earth I'll be able to contribute tomorrow.

Just as we are packing up, Heidi appears. She looks after all the logistics for the interns and tells us that Phil, who is working on the build of a Simple Survival (the smallest and cheapest of the Earthship models), desperately needs more people to give him a hand. Dale and I immediately volunteer ourselves, apologizing to Gunner, but saying he will probably get on better without us. He doesn't disagree.

I DID THAT
*

'It's all I've ever done!' laughs Phil. 'Build Earthships.' He joined Mike as a volunteer in 1992 and since then he has built Earthships all over the world. His passion is for the humanitarian work they do. He has just come back from Zuni Pueblo, a Native American reservation about five hours away, where they are building an Earthship veterinary centre, funded by donations paid by the volunteers who come and work on it. In 2018, in the aftermath of Hurricane Maria, Phil and Mike went to Puerto Rico. They teamed up with local people and together started building a community and education centre that will double as a hurricane shelter. The project is ongoing – Phil will be back there in a couple of months – and again, the funds come from donations and volunteers. The beauty of Earthships mean that so many of the materials needed – the tyres, bottles and cans – are all too easy to find locally and cost nothing. And even those with no building skills or experience can contribute. 'As long as it doesn't involve measuring or carpentry,' I tell Phil. 'Poor Gunner, I think we drove him mad.'

The house we are helping to build has been commissioned by Miriam. Miriam grew up in a small rural village in Germany, trained as a pre-school teacher and moved with her American husband and her daughter to his hometown of Santa Cruz in California. They bought an apartment with plans to renovate it, but regulations prevented them doing what they wanted and, once they started work, they discovered the apartment had been built very cheaply and badly.

'It is so important for me to have a home,' Miriam tells me, 'I think particularly because I come from another country. I need a home to make me feel rooted. But I just don't like or trust the way houses are built here after my experience with that apartment.'

Her marriage faltered and ended. But she had to stay in America for her daughter. It was a friend who told her about Earthships.

'I started to research them and I found out about the community and that I could buy a plot of land. The architectural plans for a Simple Survival Earthship are $1,600 and they are preapproved. And I thought: *Hey, I could build this house myself!*'

She didn't know anything about the area, had never heard of Taos or visited New Mexico. But she would fall asleep in front of the Earthship community map, dreaming of the plot of land she could buy and the house she could build.

Her new partner was not in favour of the idea at all, but also realized that prices in Santa Cruz made it impossible for him to buy anything there. So he and Miriam travelled down to Taos and rented the Phoenix for a night. They returned a bit later in the year, spent a bit more time.

'And we felt so comfortable here,' says Miriam. 'And when we went to look at the plot of land I'd been dreaming about for so long, we decided to buy it. We discussed with Mike what we would build and decided on the Simple Survival, but to build it in a way that would allow us to add on to it later.'

Work started in the summer while Miriam was back working in Santa Cruz. She felt like she was missing out. She wanted to be part of the plans and the building process. So she signed up for the Earthship Academy – a month-long course that involves lectures as well as hands-on experience.

'I loved it,' Miriam laughs. 'I just wanted to learn more and more and now I don't want to leave. I just want to stay until it's finished. I'm having the time of my life, really.'

What is it, I ask, that has fired her up so much, given her so much enjoyment and satisfaction?

'It's doing something meaningful. And you can just be yourself here. It's OK if you're not perfect. You can try things, find abilities you didn't know you had, and it is such a wonderful feeling.'

'So will this be the home that you felt you were missing?' I ask, and her eyes fill with tears.

'I don't know why I'm crying,' she laughs, 'but yes. I can see all the work I put into it. I built the bottle wall, cut every bottle, cleaned it, polished it, taped it. It is already a house full of memories and it will always be more special than any house I could ever buy. I don't need luxury, just this little house with the bottle wall that I made and the view.'

There's still a lot of work to be done before it's ready to move into. Phil tells us there are two pressing tasks that need to take priority – getting the first layer of adobe on the walls and the domed ceiling (*how the hell do you do that?* I wonder) and to make the greenhouse watertight.

Dale and I set to work shovelling earth through a giant hand-made sieve for the adobe mix. As the pile of fine, sieved earth grows, I feel again the simple pleasure of doing something useful. Dale mixes the adobe, but rather than me helping him and Miriam apply it, Phil says he needs me to make the metal flashings that will be bolted around the windows to make the greenhouse waterproof.

I look at him, wondering if he could possibly be serious. I thought I'd been painfully clear when I arrived on site that morning about my total lack of aptitude when it came to carpentry or anything that involved being patient and meticulous. Phil carries on regardless.

'Here's what I need you to make,' he says, handing me a flat strip of metal, the corners cut off and holes drilled at equal distances along its length. 'We need one for each window – that's eleven – and each one is bespoke. I'll give you the measurements.' I grab a notebook and scribble down the numbers as he calls them out from the top of his ladder. 'Three foot one and seven-sixteenths,' he shouts down.

'What the bloody hell kind of measurement is that?' I ask, feeling rattled already.

He gives me a rueful smile.

'Sorry! I work in inches – it'll all make sense when you look at the tape measure.'

So, with a notebook full of incomprehensible numbers and fractions, I find myself standing at a table in the winter sunshine, with several lengths of metal, a Sharpie, a tape measure, a carpenter's square, a hammer, a drill and a pair of lethal-looking metal snips. 'The man must be deranged,' I say to myself, as I take my first measurement.

By the end of the day, I've made all eleven metal flashings. I've meticulously pressed strips of black rubberized tape, which will make the waterproof seal, to each of their edges, with just the right amount of overhang (about one-sixteenth, I'm told). They are carefully numbered and laid out ready for Phil to fit.

I've also helped him install the internal windows, which involved caulking – 'what?' Caulk is the glue that holds the window into the frame. It is squeezed out of a tube, not unlike icing from a piping bag. Something else I've never done, not being a fan of icing. As a consequence, my caulking is very blobby, uneven and not remotely straight, but Phil politely ignores it and we press the window in place and hold it fast with a temporary wooden catch.

'Tomorrow I'll need you to make the strips for the bottom of the vertical windows and finish the last of the wood frames,' Phil says, as we pack up the tools.

He just assumes I can do this stuff, I say to myself, as I walk back to my car, *but maybe I can.*

THAT FRIDAY FEELING
*

It's lunchtime. Phil has gone to meet up with Mike; Miriam has headed down the road to the house she is renting while she works here; and Dale is eating peanut-butter sandwiches in his car. I've had a Thermos of soup and, knowing it will be a while before everyone is back, decide to go for a walk. From the front of Miriam's Earthship a dry water course leads your eye between the angular outcrops of grey and red rock to a tree. In a landscape almost devoid of trees, it was the view of this one that inspired Miriam to choose this particular building plot. It is a juniper. Protected by the banks of stone that rise either side of it, it is sheltered from the wind and is perfectly symmetrical, almost unnatural looking, as if it had been drawn by a child.

I pick my way between and over smooth grey stones, boggy patches of vegetation and the remains of snow that has been slow to melt in the shade of this little canyon. Small birds flutter amongst the straggly plants, their wing beats the only sound in an otherwise deeply silent world. Distances in landscapes like this are deceiving.

Two decades ago, I spent five weeks travelling almost a thousand miles across the Sahara with a train of fifty camels and three salt traders from Timbuktu. The memories of that journey are amongst my most treasured. It was a truly formative experience; at times desperately hard, but with the hardship came knowledge, profound respect and wonder. People often asked afterwards whether it was boring, just walking day after day with nothing to look at but sand. But the desert is not just sand. Nor is it featureless or monochrome. It is infinitely varied and nuanced and, because it is uncluttered by the

trappings of human habitation, because the space is seemingly endless
and I was experiencing it in an entirely immersive way, at walking pace,
unshielded even at night (we slept out on the sand), I would notice
every little detail, every rock, sand ripple, footprint. How the sun, as it
tracked across the sky, changed the colour of the land around me. How
shadows would shrink and darken, then lengthen again. How, when
we were travelling at night, as we often did, the blue of the daytime sky
would change, become eventually colourless and infinitely dark. How
the pinpricks of stars would start to appear, would get sharper and
brighter as the night deepened, how they would track across the sky,
arching above us, sweeping us along with them, making us feel part
of something vast and intangible. And at the start of every day, after
we'd drunk our glasses of black, sugary tea and loaded the camels, the
man in charge, Rachman, would point at a dune, or shrub, or a rock
in the distance and we'd walk towards it. In the early days I would try
and guess how long it might take to reach our goal, but I soon realized
that be able to judge distances in the Sahara with any sort of accuracy
would take a lifetime.

Miriam's tree appeared to be barely ten minutes' walk away, but it
took a good half hour. I walked around it, my hand caressing the rough
bark of its trunk and then walked slowly back, enjoying the view of
Miriam's Earthship, slowly revealing itself as I got closer. I scrambled
up the last incline and stood in front of it, amidst the tools, the
worktables and the neatly piled timber. That morning, I had finished
the last of the external wooden frames for the windows. The final one
had needed 'scribing' so that it would fit exactly between the edge of
the window and the wall. Phil had given me a brief lesson on how to
work out the shape I needed to cut, told me to get the jigsaw out of his

truck and have a quick practice with it on an offcut of wood before I did the real thing. It had taken a bit of honing, a bit of work with a planer to get the bottom of the frame to fit snugly, but there it was, in place, along with the other frames I'd cut and shaped and drilled. Above them, around the sloping glass that makes up the roof of the greenhouse corridor, are the metal window flashings I had made. And at that moment I get why Phil has been doing this for nearly thirty years and why Mike, at 74 years old, is still on-site every day. Why he said, in answer to my question 'Do you ever imagine stopping? Putting your feet up? Wearing slippers and watching daytime telly?' 'Well no. It would be no fun. This is fun. People go to work to make money; to a church or a synagogue or wherever for their religion; a spa or a gym to be healthy; have a hobby like golf. I get all of those things from doing this. I get my exercise, I get the money I need. It's my hobby and it's my religion! And people say – even people that are close to me – that I'm an idiot, that I could be making a shitload of money. But I'm making enough to keep going, to keep snow treads on my car in winter and food on the table, and every day is really fulfilling.'

It's rare, I muse, that people find what makes them truly happy. It seems so much part of human nature – in our culture at least – to always think there might be something better around the corner – that a bit more money, or driving a swankier car, living in a bigger house, owning a new gadget – will be the thing that brings lasting happiness. How come, I say to Mike now, he's found the answer when it eludes so many? He responds in a way that is, I now know, typical of Mike.

'I stumbled onto it, you know. I turned over a rock and there was a pearl. I didn't figure it out. Well, I did. I climbed onto a pyramid and gazed at the moon.'

This is not a euphemism. He did – I've seen photographs. In an early phase of developing his unique structures he became interested in pyramids and, being Mike, he built one. On its apex he lashed a sort of wooden box. When it was full moon, he would climb up on the roof and lie in the box to watch the moon move across the sky. And this is when, he said, thoughts and ideas for buildings that look after the people who live in them – provide them with the fundamental human needs of warmth, power, water and food – came to him.

And although he has plenty of detractors, and many throughout his working life have written him off as crazy, his buildings are still being commissioned, still being built, always with the help of volunteers like me. And it is, as Mike says, fun. It is fun to be outside in the elements, doing physical labour. It is fun to learn new skills, to challenge your perception of yourself. And it is hugely rewarding, as I now feel as I look at Miriam's house, to see the tangible, three-dimensional evidence of all those things. To know exactly what it took to make them and to be able to look down at the hands that did the work.

There is some of the same fitness in a man's building his own house that there is in a bird building its own nest. Who knows if men constructed their dwellings with their own hands, and provided food for themselves and families simply and honestly enough, the poetic faculty would be universally developed, as birds universally sing when they are so engaged.

HENRY DAVID THOREAU, *WALDEN*

A CHANCE ENCOUNTER
*

There is a great deal to admire about the Earthship concept, not least Mike's dogged determination to make it an easy, practical and attainable option for anyone who wants to live off-grid, whether for the sake of the environment, or their own finances, or both. And it is so unusual – and refreshing – to meet someone who devotes their entire working life not to trying to get rich, but doing something simply because they believe so wholeheartedly that it has benefits for society as a whole. And that would be true, I think, of everyone I met who worked at the Earthship HQ.

But after I left and had time to reflect on my experience, there were two things that niggled, that made me doubt whether an Earthship could ever be my house of the future. The first was the concern that although they work beautifully in the dry, sunny climate of New Mexico, how well would they work in Wales, which is neither dry nor very sunny for a lot of the year?

We could, of course, go and live in New Mexico, and there are many worse places to be. I really enjoyed my time there. Loved the interesting and diverse community of people who have gathered in and around Taos; the fact that they are friendly, open-minded and interested in the wider world. There are landscapes that make your heart leap, and there are chillies in almost everything that anyone cooks. But when Ludo and I talk about how and where we might spend the next chapter of our lives, we always come back to the fact that we love being here, in a country so beautiful it makes me stop dead in my tracks just to take it all in; moves me, quite often, to tears. A country where we have friends we hope will still be our friends, even when we are too old and mad to remember each other's names. Where strangers will stop for a chat, or will help you out, will be hospitable and kind because that is their nature. Wales, we realize, really is home.

The other niggle is that, although once they are built Earthships can function and be lived in with minimum negative impact on the environment, one of the principal components used to build them is concrete. Concrete is made from mixing together sand, gravel and cement, and it is cement that is the villain of the piece. Cement is the most widely used material in existence, and second only to water as the planet's most-consumed resource. It is also the third largest source of manmade CO_2. If the cement industry were a country, a 2019 article in the *Guardian* reported, only the US and China would beat it in terms of carbon-dioxide emissions.

But what is it about this dusty grey powder that makes it so damaging? Cement is made from limestone and clay or shale. Once quarried, they are crushed to a very fine powder and mixed together. The mix is then 'cooked' in a kiln at very high temperatures – between 1,400°C and 1,500°C – which produces gravel-like nodules known as clinker. When the clinker is ground up – often with added chemicals – it becomes cement. All aspects of cement production are polluting, but the chemical reaction that occurs in the production of clinker and the combustion of fossil fuels needed to run the kilns at such high temperatures create the majority of the eye-wateringly high CO_2 emissions.

While Phil and I were working on Miriam's Earthship, I raised the issue of the use of concrete with him. It is a conversation he's had many times with interns who often express the same concern.

'There are alternatives,' he told me, between mouthfuls of sandwich.

'We've used hempcrete, for example. But the advantage of concrete is that it is widely available – which is important when we are doing our humanitarian builds in more remote places. And often we are building homes or community shelters that need to be able to withstand typhoons or earthquakes, so they need the strength concrete provides. And it keeps the overall costs down. It is a conundrum, but by using waste materials to create the bulk of the infrastructure and building homes that need almost no fossil fuels to run, Earthships are, I believe, still a good option for people to live in a low-impact, but comfortable and practical way.'

Cliff Blundell suggested another option for a way to live that puts less strain on the earth's resources – and the bank account. And it was rather surprising. I met Cliff while I was working in an isolated area of Pembrokeshire and staying in a cottage just below his house. We coincided one morning in the lane that runs the length of this almost hidden valley. The lane is narrow and, other than by the few people who have farms or live alongside it, is little used. Grass grows down its middle. This being rural Wales, people talk to each other if they coincide in lanes, and when Cliff told me that he lived in the red house, I not only knew exactly the house he was talking about, but could say, with all sincerity, that I rather lusted after it. I had obviously said the right thing, because two days later I am sitting in that very house, having lunch with him and his wife Katrina.

Cliff conserves historic buildings, this house being one of them, and this is when I discover that even the word 'cement' makes Cliff splutter with indignation. Cliff has records of his house and the people who lived there going back to 1713, but it is likely there was a dwelling of some kind on this site from the 1400s. Originally it would have been just one room with a fireplace which doubled as an oven. Later, another room was added – the one we are sitting in now – making the house longer. Then, at some point, a second storey was added. It is built, like many of the traditional buildings in Wales, with thick stone walls, straight onto the earth. Between the exterior stone wall and the interior stone wall there is a gap which is filled with rubble and earth. These thick, solid wall structures have no need for concrete mortar to hold them together, nor, in common with Earthships, do they have need for foundations.

'This slate floor,' says Cliff, tapping his foot on it, 'is laid on the mud beneath the house. Modern houses, built with much thinner brick or block walls cemented together, need foundations to stop them falling over.'

'But what about damp?' I venture, because the perceived wisdom, frequently based on experience, is that houses with stone walls and no foundations are prone to being both very cold and very damp.

'Only', Cliff says, with some agitation, 'when people cover them in concrete in the mistaken belief that that is going to keep water out. But concrete is the very thing that makes these houses damp. It stops them working. It stops them breathing. It kills them.'

When he and Katrina bought this house, it was covered in thick, grey concrete pebbledash and the interior walls were plastered in cement and painted with vinyl paint. And it was, they say in unison, 'grim'. And cold. And damp. But Cliff knew that if they got rid of all the modern materials – the concrete, the cement, the paint – the house would be restored to the warm, dry refuge it had been for hundreds of years. And that is because over the time we have been building solid wall structures – about 2,500 years – we've learned that the outer layer of stone will let water in. That water is held in the cavity that is packed with earth and rubble and, as soon as the moisture level outside is lower than it is inside, the water held in the walls evaporates. Put concrete on the outside wall, cement plaster and vinyl paint on the inside walls, and any water in the cavity is trapped. It can't get out. And that's the source of your cold and damp.

Cliff and Katrina's house is still rendered on the outside and plastered and painted on the inside, but they have used lime – the material that was used on all buildings before the advent of cement in the 19th century. Lime mortar is also composed of limestone and an aggregate like sand, mixed with water. But the heat required to 'cook' it is much lower, and therefore so is the level of CO_2 emitted. The resulting lime putty then absorbs CO_2 as it cures. But its environmental attributes are a nice added extra. The use of lime is essential in the building of stone houses because it is permeable. It lets water in, and crucially lets it out again. It works like a merino wool vest, wicking moisture away and allowing it to evaporate. Concrete works like an old-fashioned oilskin. Keeps water out, but you sweat in a very unladylike way beneath it. The sweat can't evaporate, trapped as it is by the super-waterproof oilskin, so you get cold and damp. Like an old stone house covered in concrete.

Cement in its modern form came into its own post-Second World War, when the need to rebuild towns and cities ravaged by bombing was central to the new government's manifesto. Cement was quick and easy to use, whereas lime requires a great deal of skill and those skills had largely been lost during the war. Houses with concrete foundations and thin walls became the norm and, without insulation, double-glazed windows and central heating, they too are cold and damp. I'm sitting in Katrina's and Cliff's house in the middle of a winter's day.

Outside it is raining and a cold wind whips off the hills. But we are warm and dry in this old stone house, with its slates sitting directly on the earth beneath our feet. And there is no central heating. In the room where we sit is a wood-fired range 'built in 1936', Cliff tells me, with pride, that heats their water which comes from a spring on the hill behind the house. And in the room they call the parlour – the oldest part of the house – there is a woodburner in the fireplace that was once the oven. The only utility they have to pay for is electricity. Katrina, a designer and artist, mixed the lime washes that cover the interior walls, their colours enhancing the cosy comfort of the rooms. They are all inspired, she tells me, by her walks on the hill.

'They are the colours of our landscape. The bracken and grasses and fungi. And the colour on the outside of the house (which is a deep, earthy, orange red) is the same as the lichens that grow on the rocks.'

I tell them of my dream to build a house that works in harmony with the earth, using sustainable materials and without the need for fossil fuels. 'I don't need to guess that you will advise using lime, but what would be the best building materials to use?' I ask.

'You definitely want to go for a solid wall structure and avoid the need for a big concrete foundation,' Cliff replies. 'Straw bales are a possibility, and in the next few years I think we will see more people building with hemp or jute blocks. These are good, because you can harvest three crops a year of each, they absorb CO_2 while they are growing, and you bind them with lime, which also absorbs CO_2. They are very insulative – like the tyres used for the Earthships – and they don't create any waste when they are manufactured.

'But if you want to be really green, don't build a new house. Find an old one and put it right.'

Old is the New New

DUTCH COURAGE
*

Cliff's philosophy of making use of the old, rather than automatically aspiring to something new, is one that would resonate very much with Machted Regnten. Machted – 'call me Maggie' – was a creative director working in the digital industry, building and overseeing teams that created some of the biggest websites in the world. She earned a fat salary, travelled a lot, drove an expensive car. She wasn't a voracious consumer, she told me, as she sipped her coffee (no conversation in Amsterdam is possible without coffee to accompany it), but as a designer she had always enjoyed having beautiful things around her. And it was this appreciation for beautiful things, combined with a growing realization of how wasteful we are as a society, that inspired Maggie to make a dramatic change: to give up her secure, well-paid job and start her own business.

I have Baruch to thank for introducing me to Maggie and Henry to thank for introducing me to Baruch. Henry and Baruch met in their late teens – school leavers on a European adventure. Baruch, the son of an American father and Dutch mother, had something of an international childhood. He and Henry met in France at a party neither of them can remember being invited to. They've been friends for 30 years and, when I told Henry one evening, when we were gathered around his convivial kitchen table having supper, that I was going to Amsterdam to meet the woman who came up with the idea for the repair café, he said, 'You need to get in touch with Baruch.' So I did.

Baruch has had an unorthodox working life. For a decade he lived as an 'anti-squatter' in various buildings around Amsterdam and at the same time became an 'upcycler', collecting quirky lamps, posters, furniture, old sheet music, even doors and staircases, using them to refit interiors for individuals and businesses. He is gratifyingly enthused by my quest to find and meet people who have been inspired to make a shift towards simplicity, to look for other sources of contentment that are longer lasting, more satisfying and more sustainable than the quick 'happiness fixes' we chase.

We meet on our bikes outside the hotel he'd recommended in Amsterdam-Oost, a building that itself has been recycled many times. In the early 1920s it was a quarantine centre for immigrants. In 1939 it became a refugee centre for Jews, then later the Germans used it as a detention centre. It remained a prison after the war until 2001, when it became a place for artists to live and work in. Its artistic past is evident in its design today and all the rooms are individually furnished with thrift-shop finds.

We cycle to the terminal for the ferry that carries pedestrians and cyclists across the stretch of water between the central station and North Amsterdam every five minutes or so. We push our bikes into the throng of people already on board and inch our way towards the bow to allow more to get on behind us. When we reach the opposite bank, we coast down the ramp of the ferry and follow a canal, before turning on to another cycle track that takes us through a district of 19th-century apartments built for workers and their families. Ahead of us is what had once been the site of an oil depot, a swathe of flat wasteland peppered with abandoned buildings in varying stages of dereliction. But as is so often the case with areas like this (I'm thinking of London's East End and Docklands in the 80s – grimy, dilapidated, unfashionable with streets of boarded-up buildings and empty warehouses), it has attracted the artistic and experimental.

As we cycle over a bridge, Baruch waves at a small group of buildings that appear to be floating on the water below – 'You should see this!' – and we turn down a track that leads to the water's edge. We lean our bikes against a bench and I follow Baruch on to a broad wooden boardwalk that sits just above the surface of a wide canal. The boardwalk meanders between houses that appear to be floating. They have been recently built – some are still under construction – and although all different, their designs are clean and sleek. There's lots of wood and glass and each one, I notice, has a bank of photo-voltaic panels on the roof.

This, Baruch tells me, is Schoonschip, or Clean Ship, and it claims to be the most sustainable floating neighbourhood in Europe. The concept was dreamt up in 2008 by Marjan de Blok and Thomas Sykora, who, after scribbling their ideas down on a piece of A4, started to approach others to gauge what the level of interest might be in living in a floating community. This wasn't to be an 'alternative' community that existed on the fringes of society. Like Mike Reynolds and his Earthship community, Marjan and Thomas intended the idea to appeal to professionals, to families, and for them to be able to live normal, mainstream lives, just in a more sustainable way.

To be part of it required quite an investment. Each household was asked to contribute €100,000, which paid for communal infrastructure, like the boardwalk connecting the homes, the community centre and sewage disposal. The design of the homes – there are 46 of them – was up to the individual householders, but they had to be able to work off-grid and to use water sparingly. The advantage of having everyone on board before building started, Matthijs tells us as we sit in his light-filled kitchen, the water lapping at the deck outside the open door, was that it gave them buying power. Matthijs is a friend of Baruch's (who seems to know everyone, everywhere) and has built his house at Schoonschip himself.

'The good thing was that all the houses needed solar panels, they all needed warm-water pumps and, rather than buying them individually, we could buy in bulk for the whole community, which made it cheaper.'

Matthijs's wife, Nienke, comes into the kitchen in her dressing gown, rubbing her wet hair on a towel. She's just been for a swim in the canal.

'It is a wonderful way to start the day!' she says. She's a doctor and drives to her practice in a car from the hub of electric cars, scooters and e-bikes that are available for anyone in the community to use. A further idea that has recently been put into practice, she tells me, is buying food communally rather than as individuals. 'We joined forces with local producers, and now we order food for the whole community, which cuts down on waste, on transport and makes growing on a small scale more viable, because they have a guaranteed customer base.'

'What a cool place!' I say to Baruch, as we cycle on past a line of shipping containers that have been turned into artists' studios.

'It's great, isn't it? And hopefully it will inspire more communities to pool resources and collaborate the way they have. It makes so much sense.'

We stop again briefly to walk around a cavernous machine shed, complete with hulking metal remnants of its past, now being used as a place to build theatre sets. Next door is a 3-D printing business – 'They're printing a bridge,' Baruch tells me, as we cycle on, and I wonder if I heard him right.

The café where we stop for lunch is in an old storage shed – unprepossessing from the outside but inside its eclectic mix of sofas and chairs, long shared tables and mismatched benches, together with simple, unfussy food and artisan beers, attracts an achingly cool crowd, even on an ordinary working Wednesday.

'I want you to meet Maggie because she is doing what I've been thinking about doing for so long. But while I've been talking about it – with Henry, actually, because he's interested in the idea too – Maggie has gone and done it.'

We lean our bikes against the graffitied wall of a red-brick building by a handwritten chalkboard sign that reads: 'If you want something new, buy something old.' It reminds me of Cliff.

Beyond the door is a big space, airy and light. There are pot plants, pictures on the wall. It doesn't feel like a showroom – although it is – but more a much-loved private collection of miscellanea. There's a long table, hefty and handsome, built by three young designers from the salvaged steel couplings of a train and wood from a cargo wagon. There's a delicate, pretty chair, built in the 1930s, awaiting new fabric for the seat, but otherwise as good as new. A collection of coloured glass bottles sits on a small cabinet with stained-glass doors. A white plastic garden chair rescued from a skip – still in need of a clean, but the perfect find for any admirers of 80s design. A simple cupboard made in the 60s by a carpenter whose skill and pride in his work are evident in its faultless construction and longevity. And amongst these treasures sits Maggie, perched on a white painted wooden chair, working on her laptop. In a black and white striped T-shirt, short black skirt and white trainers, she wears no make-up and has a big, generous smile.

There is the ritual coffee-making before she sits back down and begins her story. It started, she tells me, when she moved into a new house. It needed quite a lot of renovation – new heating, ventilation and wiring, as well as decorating and furnishing.

'And I wanted to do it as sustainably as possible. That was my goal, but it turned out not to be at all straightforward. It involved such a big search and, in the course of that search, I realized that I wasn't just looking for sustainable ways of restoring my house, I was looking for a new way of life and the two things sort of came together. Food miles and the provenance of food has become something that many of us consider almost without thinking. The fashion industry – the waste it generates, its use of child labour to make cheap, throwaway stuff – is now being scrutinized and increasingly held to account. But as I was working on my house, it struck me that no one is thinking about the things we have in our homes, how we decorate them or furnish them. I'm a designer: I love interior design, but it is so wasteful. Think of all the household stuff you see left on the street or thrown into skips – sofas, chairs, things that might be a bit broken, or just a bit unfashionable – that can be fixed up or repurposed and given a new lease of life. So, the idea that came to me was to make it easier for people to find old or repurposed things for their homes without having to spend all that time searching, like I had to.'

'But aren't there lots of places that do that already?' I ask, thinking of the upcycling centre in my local town, where I have bought, as well as donated, furniture.

Maggie nods.

'Yes, but you have to be lucky to find what you are looking for or have the time, inclination and skill to fix or paint or reupholster the thing you want.'

I know from experience she's right, but still don't see how her proposition is different from the thousands of people selling antiques or vintage furniture in shops or online.

'My aim is to champion circular design and bring it under one roof – a one-stop shop, if you like – for anyone doing up their house. There are little start-ups here in the Netherlands trying to do something with recycled building materials. Others are curating and selling vintage and second-hand furniture and there are brands creating new products that meet the "circular" remit. I want to bring them all together, make it as easy and affordable as it is now to buy food produced locally, or products that avoid the need for single-use plastic.'

I confess at this point that I only have the vaguest notion of what she means by 'circular'. And she explains.

The Circular Economy

The economic model that drives the Western world – in fact, most of the world – is linear. We take raw materials, make something out of them and throw them away when they break or we tire of them. A circular economy does the opposite. This economic concept is based on a closed-loop system. Circular products, equipment and infrastructure are made to last longer, to extend their productivity. What would be considered and treated as waste in a linear economy is, in a circular one, repurposed or re-used or composted. This approach minimizes the use of new resources and the creation of waste and, in doing so, significantly cuts down on the pollution and carbon emissions that are part and parcel of a linear economy.

As I listen to this, it seems quite staggering that we haven't wholeheartedly adopted this idea already. Because it is not a new one. It has been germinating and taking shape for over half a century. The first person to put this concept on paper was an American economist called Kenneth Boulding, who in 1966 called for a shift away from what he called 'the cowboy economy' – one where there are no limits on the consumption of resources and waste disposal – to a 'spaceship economy' where everything is engineered to be constantly recycled.

It took until the early 80s for Boulding's idea to start being adopted. A report commissioned by the European Commission was published in 1981 and concluded that a circular economy would create jobs locally, reduce the consumption of resources, carbon emissions and waste. Those are all good things – beneficial to every one of us. And there are companies – big companies as well as start-ups – that have adopted the circular approach. British company Winnow has developed smart meters for use in commercial kitchens to reduce food waste. Their monitors, where used (and they have been adopted in kitchens in 40 different countries now), reduce waste by 50 per cent and save companies millions. US-based HYLA Mobile works with many of the leading manufacturers of smartphones and tablets to repurpose or re-use either the devices or their components, preventing 6,500 tonnes of e-waste ending up in landfill. And yet the linear economy persists and furniture is one of the fuels that keeps it going. Every year, Europe discards 10 million tonnes of furniture and most of it ends up in landfill or is incinerated. In 2015 FIRA (the Furniture Industry Research Association) launched a research project to look into the measures required by UK furniture manufacturers to enable them to adopt a circular-economy approach. This was in response to the shameful facts that in Britain we consign 1.6 million tonnes of furniture to landfill annually and a horrifying 80 per cent of the materials used to make that furniture ends up as waste.

Zen and the Art of Being Circular

The time, effort and determination that Maggie had to adopt to turn her house into a physical manifestation of the circular economy proves that the idea still has a long way to go before it becomes mainstream. But she repurposed, re-covered, repaired. She made all her curtains and cushions, but with the extra challenge of using only second-hand fabric and not buying anything new.

'I came up with a trick of making curtains out of strips of cloth rather than just one big piece – which is so dull. It meant I could use offcuts and end-of-roll scraps and they look beautiful. And it's a Zen thing to do, making things by hand.'

She taught herself to sew when she was 12.

'I was very self-conscious and I wanted to look good. I didn't get money from my parents for clothes, so I had to be creative.'

Her mother had a sewing machine she didn't use, so Maggie had it in her room.

'I used to hide behind that sewing machine for hours. I still do. It relaxes me. It eases my mind. You have to work at an even pace, to focus and concentrate. It's very meditative.'

She can't imagine ever going to buy a new, mass-produced piece of furniture again.

'I love the treasure hunt, finding something that someone regarded as waste and thought was worthless. I love the process of cleaning it up, of fixing it, uplifting it, making it unique. It's putting the sunshine back into it. That's what is so fulfilling. It is why I called my business Sirkuler Design. It's the way I now live. And I'm much happier, more relaxed, more mindful. I have a lot less money' – and she grins a little ruefully – 'and I do need to make this work financially, but I believe in what I'm doing. I think we are at the stage now when people do want to live more sustainably, are ready to adopt the idea of a circular economy and make it their way of life.'

'Is there anything about your old life you miss?' I ask, as I pack up my notebook.

'My Audi!' and she laughs, a little guiltily. 'But I have a bike. I cycle an hour every day. So, I'm much fitter!'

PINS AND NEEDLES
*

I envy Maggie's passion for sewing, her ability to lose herself for hours. I have an image of her sitting amidst baskets overflowing with colourful streamers of fabric, her foot on the pedal driving the machine as her hands guide and slide the material towards the rhythmic thrum of the needle. And on her face an expression of pure serenity. It is not like that for me. The very thought of sitting down in front of a sewing machine induces quite the opposite of zen-like calm.

When I see a bobbin, the reels of coloured thread, the pins, patterns, a tape measure, I see only the potential for chaos – for things being dropped, lost, getting hopelessly, eternally tangled. For fingers to be pricked, patterns to be torn, scissors to cut the wrong thing. And fabric is so enticing with all its colours and textures and patterns until you have to choose it. Then the panic sets in, a thousand questions crowd the mind. *It looks lovely on the roll, but how will it look made into a shirt/skirt/cushion? Will it hang right? Feel right? Will it go with the things I want it to go with? Would this colour be better? Perhaps not a pattern?* And so on.

I partly blame Mima, with whom I went to school. We've known each other since we were 11 and to this day it is a mystery to me why we became friends. Because she could do – apparently effortlessly – the things I longed to be able to do. In our art classes, while I would labour with such care and concentration over a still life, only to produce a static, characterless representation of a jug, an apple and a vase of flowers, she would take a piece of charcoal, scribble a few carefree lines and the result would be worthy of hanging on a gallery wall.

And then there was needlework. The very word still makes me shudder. We were tasked with making a skirt. We were given the pattern – it was, inevitably, given the rather Victorian sensibilities of our school, a pattern for an impossibly frumpy A-line skirt of mid-calf length. This was the 80s and we were teenagers. We wanted leg-revealing pencil skirts or miniskirts, slits up the back or sides. But at least the choice of fabric was up to us. I went with my mum to a department store to get it.

My mother is a woman of many talents, but sewing isn't one of them. When, as a child, I was invited to fancy-dress parties, I always went as a ghost (sheet over head with holes cut for eyes). It is probably why I have developed a life-long hatred of fancy dress. Lost buttons on school shirts would be replaced by any button she could find, sewn on with any colour thread, often not quite in the right place and, more often than not, would fall off by the end of the day. And I've never witnessed greater delight than when Mum discovered you could get name tags that could be ironed on rather than sewn.

So there we were in the fabric section of a department store, looking bewildered. A kindly assistant took pity on us and gently steered us away from the upholstery fabrics we were considering to the ones more suitable for this wretched skirt. I gazed at the rolls on the floor-to-ceiling racks, incapacitated by choice. The assistant tried making some gentle suggestions, pulling out a few of the rolls and unravelling them on the big cutting table with the deft movements of someone who does this all the time. I looked at all of them helplessly. Tried mimicking the way she rubbed the material between her fingers to get the feel of it. I simply couldn't visualize these waves of unfettered fabric being something I could wear, and how it would look cut, shaped, hemmed and wrapped around my unwilling waist. It didn't help, I suppose, that I was not much given to wearing skirts, apart from at school. I was – and still am – someone who feels infinitely more comfortable in trousers.

In the end I plumped for a very plain, bottle-green material that had a cheap, rather nasty sheen to it. Exactly, I realized, as I wrestled it beneath the foot of the sewing machine, the same colour and texture as my school skirt. And the end result was even uglier. I made it straight rather than A-line, put a defiant split in the back. It didn't help. Mima, in the meantime, had made a beautiful, swishy skirt in vibrant colours and skipped around the classroom looking glorious. If I didn't love her as much as I did – and still do – I'd have attacked her with the pinking shears.

But the urge to create with needle and thread and some beautiful scrap of fabric found at the bottom of a box in a thrift shop lurks beneath the fear. As does the pure frustration of being incapable of fixing something that seems so simple, like a broken zip, or as straightforward as shortening a pair of trousers. Luckily – and these days increasingly unusually – there is a sewing shop in my local town, staffed by a rota of cheerful, capable women who remain unfazed by any sewing-related conundrum. It is to them I flee with alterations and repairs – some of them embarrassingly minor.

It is a lovely space, full of the hum of sewing machines, colour and the sweetshop temptation of haberdashery. I always think of my grandmother – my mother's mother – when I stand in front of the racks of buttons and ribbons. I don't remember her being much of a sewer either, but she had a sewing box – an old tin full of treasures that I would play with for hours. Saved pieces of ribbon, pingy lengths of elastic, a pin cushion stuck with pins that had different coloured heads.

There was a slightly battered thimble, a tiny pair of scissors, needles between soft pieces of card, buttons in every shape, size and colour.

Watch almost any costume drama – any adaptation of a Jane Austen or Brontë sisters' novel – and there will be a scene involving the female characters perched primly on little velvet-covered chairs, embroidering handkerchiefs or doing needlepoint, unimpeded by the fact that the room is lit only by the guttering light of a few candles and the ever-present fire in the grate. It is in a scene reminiscent of this that I find myself one afternoon. And at first, I feel so out of place, so alien, I pinch myself to be sure that I'm not having some weird out-of-body experience.

There are eight women sitting on sofas and an old chaise longue around the comforting warmth of a woodburning stove. There's a tray of mugs and a teapot balanced on a pile of magazines, sewing baskets on the floor. Everyone has a garment or a piece of cloth in their laps and a needle between their fingers. The light comes, not from candles, but through large windows that overlook trees and fields, and the conversation does not revolve around the marriageability of the local gentry or what we might wear to entice a proposal from the chinless-but-wealthy visiting nephew. The talk is of sewing and how a young Frenchwoman used her skills with a needle to become part of a small community in the depths of rural West Wales.

Camille Jacquemart grew up in Marseille. Her parents divorced when she was ten years old and she lived mostly with her mum and her sisters. Early on, she developed an interest in clothes, in texture and shape. One of her grandmothers was a dressmaker, her other taught Camille to knit, but she wasn't interested in making. She was interested in design and the degree she took she describes as very conceptual.

'I remember having a chat with the course director and he said,"don't worry about sewing. You won't need to know how to sew. You just need to be creative".'

And she was – she turned out to be rather brilliant at coming up with designs and concepts, but, as her teachers would often remark, she was no good with her hands. And this started to rankle, despite the fact that being good with her hands was not a requirement for her course.

'I thought *How dare they!* and decided that I would do an internship and learn how to make things.'

Camille did her first internship in New York, where she learned pattern-cutting and the making of garments. She then moved to London to train at the studio of Alexander McQueen and it was, she said, transformative. She did lots of experimentation with different textiles, made prototypes and built up an almost reverential respect for the technicians – the seamstresses – many of whom had been with the company since the beginning, had seen it grow, had been intrinsic to its development.

'They were strict,' Camille laughs, 'and quite scary, but I loved working with them. And it was that experience that made me realize that actually I wanted to be a maker rather than a designer.' But she was also fascinated by the materials she was working with. 'I wanted to know about cloth, how it was made, its provenance.'

She was living at this time in an old warehouse, 'and there was a scrap of land at the back and I just started gardening. I grew my first vegetables, I discovered cooking. My parents didn't cook. My mum worked all the time and we were brought up on ready meals. So suddenly I was finding all these new ways of being creative – growing, cooking, sewing – and it was at this point I realized that I wanted a different sort of life – that the fashion industry and being a designer was not right for me.'

The landlord put the rent up on the warehouse. She could no longer afford to live there so, aged just 22, she decided to leave.

'I wondered what it was like to live in the countryside. I had always lived in cities, but my first experience of gardening and the enjoyment it gave me, made me think about moving away from a city. I thought I might go to Scotland, because I was also interested in wool and I knew there were mills there where I hoped I could learn about making fibre into cloth.'

She looked into being a WWOOFer (the worldwide organization for people who want to volunteer with organic farmers and growers), but couldn't find anything in Scotland.

'But I did find something in Carmarthenshire, in West Wales, working on an organic farm with rare-breed sheep and cattle.'

It was a brave move for a young Frenchwoman, unable to drive a car and with no experience whatsoever of farming or rural life. But she loved it. She loved the quiet, the space.

'It felt like hitting a big reset button.'

She stayed on the farm for a year and at the end of it she had no fixed plan or definitive idea of what to do next. Money was not a big incentive.

'I just needed enough to live, to make it work, and I think I knew I wanted to do something connected with making or growing. Looking back now, I suppose it was quite scary! The first thing I had to do was find somewhere to live.'

After I left home I lived the fairly typical, itinerant life of the young and single. I would put the word out to friends and they might know of a floor I could sleep on or a store room I could stay in for a while. Or a few of us would all be looking for somewhere at the same time and we'd trawl the ads in the back of the local newspaper for rooms, or a flat or house we could share. It would never have occurred to me to do what Camille did to find a place to stay in Wales. 'I drew a picture of the sort of little house I thought it would be nice to live in. It was amongst trees with a path leading up to it. A house from a children's storybook! And I put the picture up in the village shop with a note saying: "I'm looking for a house like this."'

And – remarkably – someone called her and said, 'We've got a house just like that.'

It was, she says, a bit of a mad move. The cottage was in the woods – a 15-minute walk from the road (she still didn't drive). It hadn't been lived in for years. There was no bathroom and no loo. But the rent was £50 per month and she spent the summer there, putting together a plan that she hoped would allow her to make a living and stay in Wales.

'There was a bursary available for young entrepreneurs and I applied. My eventual goal was to create a brand of children's knitwear, but I also loved the idea of making and teaching. And I was living in the middle of nowhere, I knew no one, so I thought if I could offer to teach people to sew, I'd make friends, become part of a community.'

She had, she says, no choice but to make it work, even though the idea of teaching gave her sleepless nights and she didn't know if anyone would be interested in learning to sew anyway. She got her driver's licence and started a mending service for her local village. She put up flyers for classes she offered in the community hall in Carmarthen. She did a local craft fair, expecting loads of people to come.

'But of course, it was a small village – there weren't many people! But there is a really good spirit in this area and there were people I met who wanted to support a young person who had chosen to move here, which was amazing.'

Her first students were people in their forties and fifties. Most of them had learned to sew at one time or another – from their mothers or at school – but hadn't done it for a long time and just liked the idea of trying again. And then younger people started coming, people who had never learned to sew. Both groups were encouraged, Camille thinks, by not just the desire to make or mend things rather than throw them away, but also the social aspect, the chance – the excuse – to get together.

It has been something of a lifesaver for Sharon, who is part of the little group today. Like me, Sharon had developed a deep-rooted fear of sewing, but for a much more understandable reason. Whilst in a sewing class at school, she got distracted and ran the sewing machine needle over her finger. Her teacher managed to detach the needle from the machine and sent Sharon to the school nurse to have the needle pulled out.

'The pain was so extreme,' she told us, 'I almost wished she would just leave the needle in place. It put me off sewing for the next 40 years.'

'Why on earth did you start again?' asked someone, as we all looked at her with horrified admiration.

'I was working in a shop in Carmarthen and Camille came in asking if she could put up a poster advertising her sewing class. And I just thought: *I want to do that*. So I went along and I was very nervous, sitting in front of a sewing machine again after so long. Camille taught us how to make a drawstring bag and I loved it. As soon as I got back on the machine, all my fear went away. I was whizzing along! So I went to her next class and made an apron. Then I made dresses, and more bags and aprons and wallets and I started to sell them. It became a huge and important part of my life, because' – and here she paused and looked at us all a little tentatively – 'because I suffer from really severe depression and anxiety. I hide it – I don't tell anyone. I don't think even my husband or my child know. But I don't really leave the house apart from to walk the dog. So that is why my sewing is everything to me. It helps calm the constant chatter in my head. And it gets me out. I can cope with being in a group like this if I'm distracted by sewing.'

Camille gives her a huge smile. Petite, in pink shirt and blue trousers, her thick brown hair escaping its pins, she has that enviable ability to make everyone feel instantly comfortable. This is a short afternoon lesson to fit between lunch and the school run and Camille stands amidst us holding a stripy sock with a large hole in the heel and a wooden 'mushroom'. I am instantly reminded of a short, beautiful scene in an Almodóvar film where Penélope Cruz plays a beleaguered wife running away with her young son. She is sitting on a bench in a railway station with her few belongings piled around her. She wraps her son in a blanket and, while he sleeps, she reaches into her sewing basket and draws out a wooden egg over which she puts a sock with a hole. Darning suddenly has a whole new allure.

Camille's small, nimble fingers demonstrate how she creates a web of stitches 'like a weaving frame', which can then be filled in with stitches going the other way. The wooden mushroom over which the sock is stretched stops her from sewing the two sides together and helps the sock retain its shape. I don't have socks that need mending, but a much-loved jumper – grey cashmere with the design of a pink and green cactus on the front. It has three small holes near the neckline at the back. I don't know how they got there – moths, perhaps, or I might have snagged it on something – but my fear is that the holes will grow and the jumper unravel. Camille tells me I can do two things – an invisible mend or make a feature of the holes. I look at her, not really understanding what she means.

'The main thing is to stop the hole spreading and the best way to do that is to use a small blanket stitch around the edge of the hole, but if you do them in different coloured threads, rather than one that matches the jumper, they become a unique part of the jumper's design.'

I like this idea and Emily, sitting next to me changing the buttons on a charity-shop cardigan she has found, says, 'I've got the perfect thread – try these!' In her basket are twists of embroidery thread in vibrant colours and there is a green and a pink that are identical to the colours of the cactus on the front of my jumper. 'Really?' I say to Camille, and I get that big reassuring smile as an answer.

I am wearing the jumper now and if I reach with my hand just over my left shoulder, I can feel the three holes, contained by the stitches I made, two edged in green and one in pink. The stitching is a little uneven, but it doesn't spoil the fact that this jumper has been given a whole new lease of life. And it's now a one-off. And it reminds me of that happy afternoon, sewing and chatting, and the sense of pride I felt when I held up the jumper that I had fixed myself. Once Camille had threaded the needle for me...

All Together Now

Simple Pleasure #7

— MAKING SOMEONE SMILE —

One of the things that I enjoy most about being older is feeling more able and more comfortable to say what I think. This doesn't mean I take pleasure in being insulting or rude – it is actually quite the opposite. As a nation we are, by nature, quite self-deprecating, and maybe it's because of this that we are not very good at giving compliments. We worry that they may be misconstrued, sound insincere or – worse – sarcastic. But nowadays, instead of just thinking that someone is wearing a beautiful dress, or has a handsome dog, or is doing their job particularly well, I tell them.

I'd been working at an evening event in London and, because it finished too late for me to go home, the organizers put me up in a hotel afterwards. It was close to Regent's Park, so when I woke up in the morning, I went for a run. It was during the first weeks of summer, the sun was out, the sky cloudless and the park was looking lovely: pristine lawns, borders full of flowers, big shady trees, birdsong and scampering squirrels. It was early and I was there at the same time as the workers who come in before most people are up, to empty the litter bins and clear up the rubbish that the thoughtless few leave scattered and abandoned.

There is a man ahead of me in the regulation green uniform, meticulously picking up litter, scouring the flowerbeds for anything that might have blown in and got trapped amongst the leaves. He is, it seems to me, not just taking great care, but great pride in what he's doing. *And he should be proud*, I think. So as I draw near, I push away the thoughts that he might not want to be approached by a red-faced, slightly sweaty stranger, or that he will think I'm weird or mad, and I pause, trying not to pant, and tell him: 'The park is beautiful. Thank you.'

'We do our best,' he says. And smiles. A big, wide smile that makes his eyes crinkle and his whole face light up.

I run on. And I'm smiling too.

*

HOW TO BE HAPPIER –

A SIMPLE SOLUTION THAT'S RIGHT ON THE DOORSTEP
*

Of all the means which are procured by wisdom to ensure happiness throughout the whole of life, by far the most important is the acquisition of friends.

EPICURUS

Camille confessed to me about 'the bit of a wobble' she had. We were carrying mugs back to the kitchen after everyone had left, and she told me that last year, around the time she turned 30, she started to be overwhelmed by feelings of insecurity.

'I had this recurring thought that I had done everything the wrong way around. The lovely time I had spent learning my craft didn't give me any financial security. But the people who were coming to my classes, seeking a way of life that allowed them the creativity and freedom they hadn't had in their work, already had a flat or a house, a pension or some savings. I don't have any of those things.' She went on to recall her time when she was working on the farm, when she knew nothing and nobody; finding the house in the woods, walking two hours to move in, with everything she owned in a backpack. 'I look back now and can't quite imagine how I did that! But then I had literally nothing to lose and everything to gain, so it was really exciting.' And she made the observation that when you have more things it can make you feel less secure rather than more so. Because you want to hold on to them. In the years since she decided to settle here, she has, naturally enough, accrued more possessions. She rents her house, but the things in it belong to her. And that is what scared her, the feeling that her existence was too precarious, her foundations too rocky, that she might lose those things that are, in some ways, her roots, the reason she stays here. 'And I got scared. And started wishing I had a proper job.'

To help her navigate these unsettling feelings, she joined a women's group and they met once a month. And it was these gatherings that made her realize that her foundations, far from being rocky, were absolutely solid.

'My security is my community: the sewing community I've built up and the people I've got to know and love around here. That is the best safety net anyone can have. So now I've stopped panicking and I'm really enjoying providing an excuse and a reason for people to get together to learn, to talk and to make things.'

A report published by the Office of National Statistics in 2018 found that 2.4 million British adults of all ages suffer from chronic loneliness. It has long been established that loneliness is linked to a number of psychological problems like alcohol and drug abuse, eating disorders and depression. But leading loneliness researcher John Cacioppo discovered the hugely significant fact that loneliness is fundamentally a biological problem and significantly increases the risk for premature mortality. This loneliness epidemic – which is how he described it – has occurred, he believes, because humans are deeply social animals and yet modern society has moved away from the community-based life for which we were, 'like ants or bees', designed.

Social media gives the illusion of community – makes people think they are connected and part of something – and in a way, they are. But nothing beats real contact. You can only tell how someone is doing by hearing their voice or, better still, seeing their face. Comfort comes –

proper comfort – from the holding of a hand or a big, squeezing hug. Small personal triumphs, little breakthroughs, should be shared and celebrated. Doubts, despairs and sadnesses can be given a new, perhaps more dealable-with, perspective if talked about with someone who can put the kettle on, push a box of tissues your way and just listen. Give undivided attention. Laughing on your own is rarely the glorious, shoulder-shaking, tears-rolling-down-the-face abandon that it can be with other people. And there are few things more restorative than a good laugh.

My own mum and dad lived in their community for over 30 years. Mum has always been someone who gathers people up of all ages, invites them in, introduces them to others she thinks they will like. Over those three decades lots of people have moved away and new ones moved in and Mum was often the person who would help them settle in. When Dad was ill and Mum was spending hour after stressful hour driving between appointments with doctors and specialists or visiting dad in hospital, I would turn up with bags of easy food to stock her fridge and freezer, only to find them already stuffed to capacity by her friends and neighbours. I was thoroughly trounced by James, her next-door neighbour who is a wine merchant. We arrived on Mum's doorstep at the same time one evening, me with a bag of M&S salad and he with a case of rosé. Mum was far more delighted to see him.

And then Dad died and, if I hadn't appreciated the importance of being part of a community up until that point, I was now reminded over and over again, by the kindnesses, the generosity, the thoughtfulness and the help with practicalities that were showered on us, unasked for. I did wonder, briefly, whether Mum might want to come and live with or near me, once things had settled down a bit, but it became abundantly clear very quickly that (a) I would drive her mad and (b) she had the best possible support network on her doorstep and a far more active social life than I have. She is so busy these days, I have to book in advance to get a chance to see her. And hooray for that.

Today I'm in a car, travelling down the M5. Janet is driving and I'm in the passenger seat, trying, without much success, to resist the little stash of chocolate toffees she keeps in one of the cup holders.

'I heard about something at the weekend that I thought might interest you.' Janet is a mine of information and always has a good story to tell. Now in her early sixties, she is a professional driver, but as a teenager she joined the police force. One of the first times I met her, she had me in fits of laughter, then full of admiration, when she told me how it had been her that had effected the change in uniform regulations that allowed WPCs throughout the force to wear trousers.

'When I joined, we had to wear skirts, with a shirt and tie, stockings and court shoes.' Janet snorts derisively. 'Not very practical, particularly when you are short, like me, and you have to climb over railings to get to someone who has jumped off the Avon Bridge.'

I reach for another toffee. This is going to be good.

'I jumped up onto the railings, but I couldn't get my leg over' – now we both snort – 'because my bloody skirt was too tight. I'd been going on and on at the Super for ages about how we should be allowed to wear trousers so we could actually do our jobs properly, but this was the early days. The 70s. Policewomen had only recently been given duties beyond looking after women and children or doing admin in the office. You don't need to wear trousers to do any of that. Anyway, the top of the railing went through my skirt and I get completely stuck. Oh, it was embarrassing! And of course the skirt has ridden up, so everything's on display and I'm helpless, can't do anything. Then along came two of my fellow officers. Two burly blokes, who obviously just have to leave me where I am, because there's this person with terrible injuries that needs dealing with first. It's only when they get him in the ambulance that they come back, shaking with laughter, and lift me bodily off the railings. I've never been so mortified. That was it. After that incident the Super relented and the rules were changed.'

Today she tells me how she spent the weekend with a friend in Dorset 'and her husband has become part of a Men's Shed'. I look at her quizzically. 'It's an organization, apparently, I think it started in Australia. But this one was set up by the men themselves.'

'And what is it?' I ask. 'Or what does it do?'

'It's a sort of club, I think. Most of the members are retired, and when men retire they tend to be at a bit of a loss and can often be quite lonely, so the shed – I don't think it is literally a shed – is a place where they can meet up and socialize, but they also do things for the community. Most of them are quite handy, so they do small jobs for people in the village – putting up shelves, changing washers on taps, that sort of thing.'

I have a brief vision of the men in this Dorset village as elderly super-heroes, their Y-fronts outside their slacks, armed with rawlplugs and a spirit level, but I banish it. Because I'm captivated by this idea, which seems to be a gloriously simple and effective solution to many of the things that blight communities today.

Back at home, I looked into it a bit more and was astonished to find that this Men's Shed wasn't just a quirky local initiative unique to that village in Dorset, but a UK-wide movement. It originated, as Janet rightly remembered, in Australia in the mid-1990s in response to a lack of opportunities within communities for men to get together and socialize. The first one to be established in England was in Cheshire in 2008, set up by the charity Age UK, and the first to be organized and established by a community was in Camden in 2011. Now, in just over a decade, there are over 500 Men's Sheds all over the country. They are individually funded, either by the communities themselves or they become registered charities.

Some have just a handful of members – or Shedders, as they proudly refer to themselves – and are open one afternoon a week. Others may have 70 or more members and are open throughout the week, as well as during evenings and weekends. The majority of Shedders are retired men, but a small percentage are younger – in their twenties or thirties – and despite the name, not all the Sheds are exclusive to men. Some allow women to join, too. And the place they meet is not always a shed. It's just somewhere that is affordable and local enough that everyone can get to it easily. A Portakabin can be a Men's Shed; so can an old warehouse or a garage. Boats have been used. Even, in one instance, a disused mortuary.

The one I'm on my way to today is an old chicken shed on a farm on the outskirts of Street in Somerset. The Street Shedders used to meet in an empty shop in the town, but the landlord decided not to renew their lease, so they had to find a new base. This, Laura tells me, is one of the biggest challenges of starting a Shed – finding premises. Laura is the person I tracked down to find out more about Sheds and perhaps even wangle an invitation to visit one. If anyone is an advocate for doing a job they love, it is Laura. Her enthusiasm is palpable, even down the phone.

'You can't possibly be unhappy doing a job like this,' she laughs. 'It is the most uplifting job in the world!' She is keen I come to Street because 'they've had a bit of a tough time. They had everything set up – an amazing workshop, and they'd got really well established and then they had to find somewhere else to go. For a while they thought they might just have to close, but then a farmer offered them a chicken shed he wasn't using. They haven't been in long, but they've achieved so much already. I'd love you to see what they've done.'

So here I am, driving up a rutted lane to a collection of farm buildings and sheds, and outside a long, low, slightly tatty barn is Brian.

'Come on in!' he says.

Inside, it is anything but tatty. I follow him into a big workshop, neat as a pin, benches and tools all in immaculate order, a rocking horse under repair in the corner.

'This is Graham's domain. You'll meet him now.'

And we go through a door at the back of the workshop into another room where there is a kitchen and a long table (they made it out of old doors), covered in a white cloth and laden with mugs, biscuit tins and a large Victoria sponge already missing several slices. Around the table sit a dozen or so men of various ages, all yacking away.

'You'd never guess,' says Brian, as he points out a free chair and hands me a mug of coffee, 'that a couple of years ago nobody here knew anybody. Even though we all live in the same village and very close to each other, not one of these gentlemen knew the gentleman he is now sitting next to. There were plenty of groups for ladies, like the WI and Knitter Natter' – which was new to me but then I'm no knitter – 'but we men didn't have anything at all and it was obvious that we needed something.'

'So was it you who started it?' I ask.

'No! It was my wife's friend, Vicky.'

'But I thought the whole point...' and I tail off as Brian laughs.

'I suspect most of the Men's Sheds in the country have actually been set up by women. Vicky asked me if I'd like to be involved because of my background. I'm terribly organized, I love organizing things. I'd been the Street Neighbourhood Watch Chairman for nearly 20 years and had recently resigned. I think my wife suspected that I was feeling a bit – well, lost – and suggested to Vicky that I might be interested in running this.'

The first meeting they held attracted 40 or 50 people. They got together in a room at the back of the local skittle alley. A few weeks later, when it was evident that people were already relying on the Men's Shed for the company and camaraderie it offered, they took on the lease of an empty shop in the high street. Brian thinks the appeal is that a Men's Shed offers more than 'an evening sitting at a bar and drinking. There's the social interaction but it is also about transferring skills. We've got some fantastic woodworkers here and they are helping teach the rest of us to make things – stuff that the community needs.'

At this point another man, Stuart, chips in.

'Most of us were coming up to retirement age or older – a stage in our lives when we needed to do something because, if you don't have any hobbies or interests at home, you need something to fill your time otherwise you end up vegetating a little. This has helped an awful lot of people. We're learning new skills – woodwork, building things, fixing things – and having something to keep you active in body and mind, and a place to come and make new friends, keeps you alive. Gives you a reason to get up in the morning.'

Graham, a remarkably spry 80-year-old – 'I married a woman 12 years younger than me, which helps!' – is a cabinetmaker and furniture designer. And it was his wife who pushed him to join, not just because she thought he would enjoy the company, but also because she knew he'd like using and sharing his skills. They had been asked by a local organization if they could make some children's benches and it was Graham who did some sketches and started to make them, using old scaffolding planks and odd bits of timber. His apprentice was Trevor, who at 68 had never done any woodwork before. He'd been a meter reader and after he retired felt, he told me, 'like a spare part, looking around for something to do'. He glows with pride as he tells me how he and Graham made the benches. 'We didn't just nail them together, we did proper jointing, put some effort into it.'

Although we all laugh about the fact that so many of the men here have come because they've been persuaded to by their wives – 'I didn't want to come at all,' joked David, 'I thought it was just going to be a lot of old farts sitting around in chairs sucking their gums' – there are some here who have lost their wives. For them, the Men's Shed has been a place of respite. A lifeline.

'It can be hard to talk to family, to your children,' says Steve, 'because they're grieving too. And they're busy, they're working all week. But I was coming home to an empty house. Turning the key in the lock and feeling the loneliness come flooding back. When I joined the Shed I was able to talk to people who understood and if I was miserable it didn't matter.'

Mike, the group's treasurer – 'he's the only one of us who can add up' – lost his wife two years ago.

'I come here, feeling a bit low, but pretending everything is OK and someone will always ask, "Are you all right?" Knowing there are people who care, who've got your back, makes all the difference.'

For 86-year-old John, the oldest in the group, the Shed has been what he describes as 'my life jacket'. Dapper, in a dark blue blazer with a brass-topped cane, he'd been the local policeman, and was well-liked within the community. Six years ago, his beloved wife Carolina died. As he says her name, tears pour down his cheeks and for a moment he can't speak. 'You're all right, John,' someone says, quietly, and he regains his composure. His neighbours rallied round, offered to cook for him, help with the garden, but despite their kindness life without Carolina was unbearable and John sank into a deep depression.

'My daughter persuaded me to go and see a doctor, and I went, but she suggested anti-depressants and I knew they weren't the answer.' So he did nothing and his health and state of mind quickly deteriorated.

In 2013 the Campaign to End Loneliness polled a thousand GPs and found that at least one in ten of the patients they saw a day came in simply because they were lonely – and in some practices it was many more than that. One GP said, 'We see people come to talk at the front desk just to pass the time of day. It's become very much part of our role here, to be a place that is welcoming and warm because the safety nets and structures in these people's lives are so skinny.' Increasingly, GPs are adopting an approach of social prescribing – where patients are referred to community-based services and programmes, which are often found to be a much more effective way of helping people like John.

'I went back to the doctor and saw a different GP this time. I told her I didn't want to take drugs and she said what I needed was company.' He left with a 'prescription' to join the Men's Shed. 'And I can't tell you, Kate. These men...' And he tears up again. 'I don't contribute a lot and I feel a bit guilty because I think I'm using them, but they saved my life.'

At this point Stuart jumps in.

'It's a pleasure having John here because he's one of the funniest people we've got. He has us in stitches sometimes with stories from his police days. And that's the thing. You don't need to come here with a skill. You can just come for tea and biscuits and a chat. We all look out for each other and we all help each other.'

'This is my sanctuary,' says John. 'It's given me a sense of belonging, a sense of well-being and the sense that all these men here – they care.'

I bid them goodbye, leave behind the banter and the laughter, the cake crumbs and custard creams, the care and support that are synonymous with this remarkable organization. Research discovered that attending a Men's Shed has seen an 89 per cent decrease in cases of depression, a 75 per cent reduction in anxiety and a 24-fold reduction in loneliness. Shedders felt happier, more focused, with a new sense of purpose. 88 per cent said they felt more connected to their community and a staggering 97 per cent made new friends. And they make their visitors feel pretty good too. I drive home feeling buoyed up and optimistic and very full of cake. 'No wonder you love your job so much,' I tell Laura, when I write to thank her.

Simple Pleasure #8

— I GOT LIFE —

The road is empty, all the windows are down, my hair blowing, the radio on. Through the speakers comes the unmistakable voice of Nina Simone. She is singing 'Ain't Got No – I Got Life', surely the most life-affirming song ever written. I turn the radio up full blast and sing my heart out.

*

COMMUNITY SPIRIT –

THE SIMPLE POWER OF PEOPLE

*

The Welsh Mill is something of a misnomer. For a start it is not, nor ever has been, a mill. It is also not in Wales, but in the English county of Somerset in a town called Frome. It was once a vinegar factory and then the base for an engineering works. Now it houses a number of small independent businesses – mainly makers. There's a master leatherworker; the Bicycle Academy that teaches people how to make bike frames that are then sent to Africa; but it is also the base for an initiative called Edventure.

Frome has been receiving quite a lot of attention in recent years. In 2019 it was in the Top 10 Places to Live in the Southwest, according to *The Sunday Times* – a year when 'community spirit' was, for the first time, one of the criteria taken into account. This seems a little odd to me, but apparently schools, house prices and internet speeds were always considered the more important factors dictating the desirability of a place to live. Frome has an independently run council that has managed, despite countrywide austerity measures, to improve the services and facilities of the town, while other councils have been hamstrung and incapacitated. But it also made the headlines for another reason, one that truly deserves shouting about. The *Guardian's* report was entitled 'The Town That's Found a Potent Cure for Illness'. And the *Telegraph* asked, 'Is Frome The Least Lonely Town in Britain?'

In 2013 Dr Helen Kingston, Senior Partner at Frome Medical Practice, joined forces with Dr Julian Abel, director of an organization called Compassionate Communities. Data published in 2018 showed the results of that collaboration. At a time when emergency admissions to hospital throughout Somerset rose by 30 per cent, in Frome they dropped by 15 per cent. The success was attributed to adopting the routine use of 'the most effective intervention for improving health and longevity, which is social relationships'. Or, as George Monbiot put it with his characteristic pithiness in his *Guardian* article, 'a new-fangled innovation called community'. It is kind of a no-brainer, but humans have a strange tendency to overlook the screamingly obvious, even when it can make our lives better in so many ways. And social connectedness (as it is called in medical circles) has been proved to have a bigger impact on health than giving up smoking, reducing excessive drinking and reducing obesity. Not that that means that as long as we are with our mates, we can all eat double cheeseburgers washed down with gin and rounded off with a packet of fags.

The joint project in Frome found a way of making 'compassionate communities' an embedded part of care. It helped people connect with existing support networks – like friends, family and community – which again, sounds obvious, but we all know how bad we can be at asking for help, even from our nearest and dearest. Yet the things they can offer – help with shopping, or cooking, walking the dog or offering lifts, make an enormous difference to someone who is unwell. And the other approach was to introduce patients to local organizations like choirs, walking groups and Men's Sheds where they can make friends and enrich their lives. And my experience at the Men's Shed in Street was testament to the efficacy of that approach.

Dr Helen Kingston said of the report's findings, 'Our project has shown clearly that we improve patient outcomes, improve working lives of the clinical teams and dramatically reduce emergency admissions to hospital. Having the community resources at hand means we can meet the needs of our patients in a way that is most meaningful to them, rather than struggling to find answers to social problems with medications.'

A significant number of the community resources in Frome originated from Edventure. I follow the signs painted on the walls up the stairs until I come to a loft-like room with a wooden floor, second-hand furniture, books and pot plants. It has the cosy informality of a student sitting room. There are a few people around. A couple on laptops, someone making coffee in the communal kitchen. Through a doorway I can see a space that looks not unlike a cave, where some sort of course or lecture is under way. A tall, slim man, in dark jeans and long-sleeved T-shirt, comes down a flight of open wooden steps from an office above and shakes my hand.

'Johannes', he says, with a slight but pronounced German accent. 'Nice to meet you.'

Johannes came to Frome via London, where he had been working with young adults, running courses giving careers advice. Some of his students were university graduates, others were older, had had children and were looking to start working again. And a recurring theme emerged with every course he did – a wish for people to find a way of working that was about more than making money.

'They wanted to carve a path towards a meaningful livelihood and make a contribution in some way. They wanted a livelihood that matters.'

'Which is what?' I ask.

'It means different things to different people. It might mean running a social enterprise or working for a socially minded initiative. For some it might be to have a stable job, that they enjoy and are respected for, but what they all have in common is wanting a livelihood that matters to them, that brings them satisfaction and contentment.'

So Johannes, together with a small group of people, started thinking about creating an education programme to support people with this goal, but location was key. It needed to be somewhere that had local entrepreneurs and a community that would be interested and willing to support the initiative.

'Our aim was to give people the opportunity to build connections within their community whilst learning in a hands-on way.' Frome, Johannes said, fitted the bill, not least 'because the generosity here is amazing. People put us in touch with other people they knew would be useful and willing to support us. Business people offered their time to come and teach. They seemed to recognize that this idea could help bring the community together.'

Edventure was born and at first it ran nine-month programmes similar to apprenticeships. Students would be given a key set of challenges that would give them the opportunity to take responsibility, initiate ideas, build their confidence and at the same time make a tangible difference to Frome – make a real contribution. The idea was honed, made more focused. The course was shortened to ten weeks and students given the task of tackling a social need – coming up with a business idea or social enterprise that was directly inspired by the requirements of the community around them.

'We think of each module as a building block. The first deals with coming up with a vision – a clear mission – and ensuring it is a common aim for everyone involved. The second is around research and enquiry. There is a lot to find out and establish before starting any sort of enterprise. The third is about working with other people to generate ideas. Then the planning phase – how to get started, what to prioritize and finally how we progress – what do we need to do or learn to move the idea forward?'

The contribution Edventure has made to its hometown in just a few short years is impressive. Johannes puts that down to the fact that every initiative has been one the community has been involved in from the idea stage: been consulted on, has understood and appreciated the benefits it will bring. And so, naturally enough, when the enterprises that developed as a result of those ideas came to fruition, they were supported. Read the articles in the press about Frome and it gives the impression that it is some sort of Utopia that revolves around picturesque cobbled streets, period houses painted in heritage colours, vegan markets and independent shops, but Frome has challenges like any community. There is poverty, social deprivation, people who need support and help in all aspects of their day-to-day lives. And that's what 'livelihoods that matter' are able to address.

There's the Roundhouse Garden, a small riverside park in the centre of Frome that has been planted with a wildflower meadow and other wildlife-friendly plants, with space to grow food for the community, as well as for art, play, relaxation, learning, exercise and gatherings. In light of the shocking dichotomy that the average household in the UK throws away almost £500 worth of food every year, while at the same time 4 million people are living in food poverty, Edventure set up The Community Fridge, the first in the UK, where residents can drop off good, unwanted food and anyone can help themselves from what's on the shelf. There's a clothing exchange and there's Share – which is one of those ideas that as soon as you hear about it, the brilliant simplicity of it, you can't believe it has taken this long for anyone to come up with it, and that it hasn't been adopted by every town in the country.

Share is run on a volunteer basis by Aliss and Sam, and I meet the two of them for coffee to find out more. Neither of them, it transpires, come from Frome originally, but the reason both ended up here says a lot about the town. Aliss was living in Manchester. She'd had a fairly peripatetic adult life, moving around with her partner's work. She had studied fashion at college, but had her children early on and never pursued it as a career. She and her partner separated and, when her children left home, Aliss, who was in her early forties, found the transition very tough. 'Not having my children around – they were my life – I didn't know what to do with myself really.'

She did some volunteer work, not feeling she had the skills to do anything else, and despite living in Manchester for eight years she felt isolated. 'The area I was in just wasn't very community minded.' She did a teacher-training course and started looking for work teaching adults. It was while visiting her sister in Wiltshire that she heard about Frome and decided very quickly to make it her new home.

'I'm very quiet and shy, but people here are so friendly and helpful. I was very ill not long after I moved here and people just came round, made me cups of tea, did my shopping and cleaned the house. I don't think that would have happened anywhere else.'

When Aliss recovered, she resolved to make a big effort, go out and do everything she could to be part of the community that had helped her so much. Volunteering was her route – 'I was on benefits then, which helped me find my feet' – and through that she started meeting people. It wasn't long before she realized that she had found her spot, a place for the first time in her adult life where she felt happy to settle. She has a studio here at the Welsh Mill where she teaches people to sew – 'young mums who want to make things for their children or older women who had bad experiences at school' – and here I nod in recognition – 'or people who've got a sewing machine but are too scared to use it. We make things for their homes or clothes.' (Aliss is wearing a pinafore dress that she made.) 'We upcycle stuff – I got lots of the old tents from Glastonbury that we made into bags.'

'My son made a lunch bag!' Lisa has joined us. She's worked at Edventure for the last couple of years. 'And he was thrilled with it. He didn't want to put it inside his school bag, because he wanted everyone to see it, so he clipped it to the outside. He was so proud!'

'It is joyful seeing people's reactions when they've achieved something,' Aliss says, with her shy smile. 'They usually can't wait to go home and make another one. It's a really good feeling.'

'And don't forget,' says Sam, 'that you also started the lantern parade! It's become a huge annual event,' he tells me. 'She teaches people to make these beautiful willow lanterns and they are paraded through the town on the night when all the Christmas lights are turned on. It's really magical. And there's a samba band and dancing and it was all Aliss's idea.'

'And what brought you to Frome?' I ask him.

'To be honest, it was because the flat my girlfriend and I were going to buy in Bristol fell through.' Sam works for himself as a website developer and writes a blog called Ethical Revolution, but he might have been a professional cricketer, had he not, at the age of 18, contracted a disease that destroyed his hip joint. He had to have a hip replacement and any hopes of a sporting career were over. After they lost the flat in Bristol, Sam and his girlfriend looked all over the place – up north as well as in the south-west. They came to Frome knowing nothing about it 'and we were walking down the street and people just said hello. People we'd never met. They were just friendly. And then I saw the Share shop and thought, *this is the place I want to be!* A few months later, we got the keys to the house we live in now. We were made to feel immediately welcome by our neighbours and have made great friends through them since. We wondered if it was a sort of "honeymoon period" but we still feel the same way now, two years later, so I guess it is real!'

'And what is Share?' I ask.

Sam smiles.

'It's a library of things, things that people in the community have donated for other people to borrow.'

'What kind of things?'

Aliss chips in now. 'Everything from roller blades to wetsuits to tennis rackets. There's event stuff like tea urns, mugs and plates.'

'Smoke machines,' says Sam, 'disco lights.'

'And there's camping gear, lots of tools and gardening equipment.'

'And how does it work?' I ask.

'There's a membership scheme that people sign up to and pay a small fee and then they pay to borrow whatever they want.'

It is, I think, a quite brilliant idea. Some people in the town use it all the time, others less frequently, but will happily borrow something for a fraction of the price it would cost to buy.

'And it works for people who perhaps don't have space to store something like a gazebo or hedge trimmers, which they are not going to use very often anyway. And lots of people like the fact that it is more environmentally friendly to have a few items that everyone shares, rather than lots of people going out and buying the same thing.'

There are, of course, those that would still prefer to buy rather than borrow, but Sam and Aliss both believe that this is the beginning of a cultural shift and that there will be an increasing move to borrow rather than to buy. The Frome Share has been open for four years and is no longer the only one in the country. The idea is catching on.

For Lisa, ending up living in Frome and getting a job at Edventure have been the vital components that have enabled her to build a new life after circumstances forced her to abandon her old one. A decade ago, she was living in Malaysia running a very successful, multi-national business, flying all over the world. She loved the work and she loved the pay packet that went with it – she was earning in the region of £10,000 a month. But her home life was not so happy. She was married, but the relationship with her husband had broken down and, although pregnant, she made the decision to leave. She returned to the UK with just one suitcase and nothing else.

For a while she was living with her mum in the suburbs of London but after she had her baby she started to look for a place that, as a single mum with an only child, would make them feel welcome, make them feel part of something. 'I wanted a community.' For a time, she and her son lived in a community in Greece. They looked at Transition towns like Hebden Bridge and Totnes. And then they came to Frome.

'And I did what my cousin and I call the "jambo" test. Years ago, when we were travelling in Africa and we arrived in a new town, we used to say hello to everyone we passed on the street, and if they didn't say hello back, we'd decide it wasn't a good place and we'd leave.'

In Frome, everyone said hello. And when she asked people if they liked living here, the answer was always yes. And so she settled here, bought a house and then wondered what on earth she was going to do to make a living. A job came up at Edventure.

'I was following them, because I love what they do on social media, so it felt like synchronicity. I went for an interview and was called back the next day for a second interview and I absolutely believed that I would be offered the job.' She wasn't. And here she was, in a new town, where she knew no one, with her son and no job. She was, she said, scared and a little bit desperate, revising her CV and looking for anything she could find that she felt able to apply for. And then her phone rang and it was Johannes, who told her it hadn't worked out with the person they had employed and would she come in for a chat? Lisa has worked at Edventure ever since.

'And how is life now?' I ask her.

'Peaceful. Simple. And I love my job. I made absolutely the right choice coming to live here.'

I turn back to Sam and Aliss.

'So would you say you've found livelihoods that matter?'

They both nod.

'My happiness is more important than earning money,' says Sam.

'I feel the same,' agrees Aliss. 'What is much more important are the people around you.'

'That's why I love living here and working here,' says Lisa. 'I can come to work every day and do something that makes a positive difference. It may be small, it may be simple, but it's good and it's practical and it's real.'

Simple Pleasure #9

— PASSING THE TIME OF DAY —

Dog and I are coming down off the hill at the end of our morning walk. For the last few days we have been staying in a tiny converted outbuilding on a smallholding. It sits on the side of a narrow valley and the view from the windows is one that makes my feet itch. Because although there are times when I am drawn to the coast, its salty air and endless horizons, I am not one of those people who dream of living by the sea. My soul needs mountains, and here the views in every direction are of rough, heathery land that falls away to a hidden stream and then rises steeply upwards. There are stiff, windblown trees, their branches reaching out in the same direction as if trying to grab at something to hold on to, and sharp, blue-grey crags of rock, like broken teeth, rising up through the soil.

Every morning at first light, dog and I leave the warm, silent sanctuary of our little cottage and, like creatures emerging from hibernation, blink at the sheer enormity of the world beyond our den. We scramble upwards, into the wind, towards the sky, pushing through thick tussocks of grass, twiggy heather and spiky gorse. Dog pronks and spy-hops, whipped into an excited frenzy by a myriad of scents and rustlings. The way gets steeper, I breathe hard and my face wants to smile, but it seems you can't puff and smile at the same time. Heart hammering, I reach the top, stand facing the wind, arms spread. 'Wheeeeeeee!' Then we make our way down by a different route, taking note of small features in the landscape that every day feels more familiar and more like our patch.

For a week I see no one on these morning adventures. All this space is ours alone. But this morning, as we are coming down the final slope towards the lane at the back of the cottage, dog barks and takes off at full lick across the side of the hill towards the line of a fence. On the other side I can see the dark silhouette of a person labouring upwards towards the ridgeline. I shout at the dog to come back – she is standing at the fence now, wagging her tail, looking for attention. I see the figure start to clamber over to my side. I wonder if they are coming to tell me off for having a dog running free on the hill, but there is no livestock about and I'm on common ground.

I start walking towards them and, as I get closer, see it is a tall man, in waterproofs and hat, the hood of his raincoat blowing wildly in the stiff, cold wind. He has the face of someone who has spent a lifetime working outdoors, a face full of character, one that is testament to hard winters and long summer days.

We reach out our hands to each other and shake – 'Morning.' Not a telling-off. Just an opportunity to chew the fat. His hand is big, rough and capable; a practical hand, one that fixes and labours. It completely envelops mine. The same hand ruffles the dog's head and she gives him a look of pure flirtation in return.

'Yours a Welsh one too?' I ask, nodding towards his dog that has stayed the other side of the fence.

'He is. Doesn't look quite as fit as yours. He's got a bit fat over the winter!'

'Haven't we all...'

We talk about the dismal weather – the storms and the huge volumes of rain that have been battering these hills all week. He was on his way to check his sheep.

'I brought them down to the lower fields and I've been feeding them sileage, but they've taken themselves back up to the top fields. We re-seeded them in the autumn, and because it's been so warm, the new grass is already coming through.'

Then there's the subject of lambing, the next big event in the farming calendar.

'We'll start at the end of March. Young chap up the lane already has some lambs.'

'I saw,' I said. 'Seems a bit optimistic to lamb so early in this part of the country.'

'I don't think he meant to. Left last year's ram lambs together with the ewe lambs too long and they obviously did a bit of practising...'

A tremendous gust of wind sweeps across the hill and bombards us with a sudden shock of hailstones. We pull our hats down hard over our ears, and our hoods up.

'Storm hasn't quite given up yet,' he shouts into the wind. 'Better get up to those sheep. See you!'

'Don't get blown away!' I shout back.

And we shake hands again and part, continuing on our solitary ways, heads tilted to avoid the stinging hail.

*

Growing and Cooking

GROWING PAINS PART 3
*

Oh, the excitement! The unadulterated joy of seeing green shoots tentatively pushing up through the soil. The first of the seeds are beginning to germinate and sprout and it really is like witnessing a small miracle. I spend quite a lot of time in the greenhouse just gazing happily at all this new life that I have had a hand in creating. It is a useful distraction from the weeding, which never seems to end, and also, thanks to the heater, it's warm in there. Too warm on occasion, which worries Emma.

The greenhouse, which gets the full, unshaded benefit of the sun for almost the entire day, is so efficient that on the days when there is sunshine, even the weak, watery sunshine of early spring, the temperature within its glass walls soars, drying out the compost and baking the fragile seedlings. And getting the balance between not watering enough and watering too much is almost impossible. Too little water and everything shrivels, too much and the atmosphere in there is akin to the Amazon rainforest and everything starts to get mouldy.

We are now the proud owners of a cold frame too. Why a cold frame should make me feel particularly grown-up and more like a 'real gardener' I have no idea, but it does. Emma has already filled it with young plants that can't cope with the heat in the greenhouse, but still need protection from the frost. I have to tuck them in with sheets of fleece at the end of the day. I had no idea that plants could be this high maintenance and time consuming, I confess to Emma. It's a marvel anything grows anywhere, ever.

No wonder weeds are so successful. They just get on with the business of growing and flowering and seeding without the need for fleece, or special compost mixes, or blow heaters. They don't need repotting – the latest task, which I manage to mostly avoid by being away working, but the little I do is tedious beyond words. They don't need feeding or talking to. I've taken to talking to the plants in the greenhouse when I'm watering them. I'm not sure it makes them grow any better, but at least it doesn't seem to be having an adverse effect. But I am having to come to terms with the fact that some of the seeds that have been planted with such care, at exactly the depth they like, in beautiful, cossetting compost, just never bother to do anything. Don't even have the courtesy to produce a single shoot or leaf. And some produce textbook-perfect seedlings, vigorous and vibrant that, for no reason and despite hours of careful nurturing, just die. Which is plain ungrateful. I'm sure gardening never looks this hard on *Gardeners' World*. Simplicity, I'm discovering, isn't necessarily simple...

In late March a parcel arrives full of what appear, on first glance, to be rather unappetizing and misshapen potatoes but are, in fact, the tubers that should produce the flouncy, fabulous dahlias of my middle-aged dreams. We plant them in big pots and put them in a shady bit of the greenhouse to wait for them to sprout. We could have waited until the final frost and planted them directly outside, but this way might encourage them to flower earlier.

Some of the vegetables that had been started in the greenhouse are ready to be transferred to the big wide world. The peas, beetroot and radishes are already in the raised beds and I transplant the feathery carrot seedlings out there too. Emma sows the broad beans and French beans directly outside. I had ordered the seeds of some pretty-looking flowers (if the catalogue was to be believed) called Calendula 'Indian Prince'. I didn't know Calendula is the Latin name for marigolds – a plant, both Emma and I agreed, that we despise. So much for my Latin A-level being useful in later life. Anyway, they grew like little troopers in the greenhouse. Emma sniffily turned down her share so I planted all of them, slightly belligerently, in the beds amongst the perennial shrubs and herbs, hoping they might get overwhelmed or just not be very noticeable. They turned out not only to be rather successful, but to add a bright perkiness that, even Emma had to concede, looked unexpectedly lovely alongside the more muted elegance of the blue, purple and white blooms that surrounded them.

'They've started!!' I write to accompany the photograph I text Emma in high excitement one morning. I've taken to checking the dahlias with the same diligence and regularity that I check my livestock and finally, finally they are showing signs of life. Tiny, almost imperceptible nodules have appeared above the surface of the compost. It's not long before these morph into stems and leaves and then proper bushy plants.

'You have to pinch the tops out,' Emma instructs.

I look at her aghast.

'Brutal, but necessary if you want shapely plants with lots of flowers.'

I get pinching. In the meantime, I had entirely given up on the gladioli that I was convinced Emma had simply buried under too much soil.

Then, all of sudden, green, sword-like leaves appeared and they shot up, only to complain bitterly about the heat of the greenhouse. But it was still too soon to risk planting them out and the cold frame isn't tall enough to accommodate their sudden growth-spurt. So they have to put up with the heat.

'Another couple of weeks and we can plant all this lot outside. Brace yourself for a lot of digging.'

Simple Pleasure #10

— FLOWERS FROM THE GARDEN —

I am wandering around the garden in a happy daze. It is midsummer and the weather, for once, is as it should be for the time of year: the sky flawless blue, the sun high and bright. Down here, in the lazy, hazy heat, accompanied by the busy buzz of a thousand industrious bees and the silent flitting butterflies, I stand in the middle of the lawn, head back, face to the sun, eyes closed, and just breathe. The air is heavy and fragrant with the smell of roses, warm soil, crushed grass. I am barefoot, relishing the extra sensory perception it gives. As a child I was always barefoot. I despised shoes and was envious and admiring in equal measure of anyone I met – or saw on the television – who could go anywhere, and walk on any surface, without them. I set myself a rigorous training regime to toughen up my soles, forcing myself to walk over gravel, trying, determinedly, not to wince and wobble. The transition to adulthood seemed to bring with it the need for footwear, and although my choice of footwear rarely involves squeezing my feet into anything that isn't flat and more-or-less foot-shaped, I still resent the fact that I have conformed.

As an aside, I did, once, just for the fun of it, try on a pair of Jimmy Choos. I wanted to see if something as spindly and strappy and delicate could really be as transformative as they are claimed to be; if by wearing them I would instantly acquire the svelte silhouette and poise of a supermodel. The shop assistant looked me up and down with unbridled distaste. Remember the scene in *Pretty Woman* where Julia Roberts has been given a fistful of cash by Richard Gere to go wild in the boutiques of Rodeo Drive, but no one will serve her? That look.

Anyway, having chosen a pair of shoes to try – and they were beautiful; far too beautiful to be stuck on a body part that no one takes much notice of – the snooty assistant slouched away to get them in my size. I, meanwhile, removed my boots and woollen socks to reveal my big, wide farmer's feet in all their bare-toed, unpedicured glory. I thought the poor woman was going to faint. I took the unwillingly proffered shoe from her hand. Cinderella or Ugly Sister? I knew what she thought. And she was right. People who wear Jimmy Choos have obviously had two, if not three, of their toes removed. No one can have feet that are naturally that narrow. I hand the shoe back. 'Sorry, not quite what I'm looking for,' I say with an apologetic smile, slip my outsized feet into the ugly, round-toed comfort of my old boots, and leave.

Today my toes are happily liberated, tickled by the grass or sinking deliciously into the warm soil as I gather flowers for the house. And what a choice I have! Emma's Bed-of-Potential-Joy, as she called it, is now, officially, The Bed of Joy, although there was nothing joyful about planting it. We carried and carted in the wheelbarrow what seemed like enough plants to create a floral extravaganza big enough to be seen from space. The dahlias – all 20 of them, with more to follow – were by now not only beautifully bushy but in bud, and needed holes over half a metre deep and as wide. Which would be no problem in most flower beds, but our soil covered, barely in places, great hunks of fork-bending, back-breaking rock. And as well as the dahlias, we had the thoroughly lanky gladioli, the lime-green tobacco plants (but no zinnia, which mysteriously failed to materialize), Emma's favourite euphorbia, cornflowers by the hundred, scabious, verbenas and the Ammi. The purple pompoms had also let us down and a plant called 'Miss Wilmott's Ghost' proved so true to its name that if it did ever germinate it faded almost instantly into oblivion.

Planting took an entire day – ten hours or so – at the end of which we didn't have the strength to stand back and admire our handiwork. Instead we lay on our backs on the lawn in a state of complete exhaustion and groaned. Anyone thinking gardening is a gentle activity useful for keeping retired folk occupied has clearly never truly gardened. And any comforting belief I had that at least the hard work was done and all I had to do now was sit on a sunlounger and watch everything bloom dissipated when the dahlias started to fall over. Such was the fabulous flounciness of the flowers they started to produce in gloriously generous profusion, they proved too heavy for the stems supporting them, which buckled and collapsed. This, I pointed out to Emma, seemed a pretty fundamental design flaw, but, as ever, she had a solution. Paul, our tree-surgeon friend and all-round man-of-the-woods, had collected a great bundle of hazel stakes for us, some of which we were using in the vegetable garden for the peas, tomatoes and cucumbers. The rest, which I carried up the hill to where Emma waited with a spade and a ball of string, were to be used to support the beautiful-but-floppy dahlias.

'These are heavy plants,' said Emma, 'so for the stakes to work, they need to be buried quite deep – about half a metre or so.' And she handed me the spade. The ground was no softer, no less rocky and Emma was uncompromising. She wiggled every stake I laboriously dug and pushed into the ground and if they wobbled, even slightly, she demanded I dig them in deeper. As days in the garden go, this was not a fun one. I started to resent Emma's insistence that things should be done properly and to despise the dahlias for being incapable of standing up on their own.

But today my labours are being amply and richly rewarded. I walk – waft, even – from bed to bed, gathering handfuls of flowers, marvelling at their intricacy, the richness and variety of their colour, and most of all the fact that they are growing in *my* garden. Not someone else's that I am wandering around enviously wishing was mine. For the first time in the years we've lived here, I feel, not *ownership* of the garden – that's not quite the way to put it. You can't *own* land in the way you own a car or a piece of furniture. You are its caretaker. But for the first time I feel that I have fulfilled my duty of care. And the flowers in jam jars on my kitchen table and in the sitting room, the flowers that I can pick, wrap their stems in newspaper and give to friends, are ones that I have chosen and sown and nurtured. Although, as I say to Emma, as I help her load her tools into her car, 'I couldn't have done any of this without your help. You're quite bloody good at this gardening malarkey. For someone so old . . .'

*

FOOD

1 – BUY IT WITH THOUGHT
2 – COOK IT WITH CARE
3 – USE LESS WHEAT AND MEAT
4 – BUY LOCAL FOODS
5 – SERVE JUST ENOUGH
6 – USE WHAT IS LEFT

DON'T WASTE IT

A US FOOD ADMINISTRATION POSTER PUBLISHED IN 1917

ODE TO AN EGG
*

It's early. I love this time of day: the world flickering its eyelids and starting to wake. I drive with my dog along the deserted road that runs alongside the river. The light is soft and grey, the colour of pre-dawn. I park up near the bridge where there is a footpath that follows the riverbank, and dog and I start to run. The air is cool, the world still and silent, cocooned in mist. The pad of my feet on the earth, in rhythm with my breathing, the only sound.

We've been running for an hour. The sun is up, flooding the world with light and colour. The mist is dissipating, the chill losing its edge, the first tentative birdsong a melody to accompany the steady beat of my steps. Dog and I scatter glistening, sun-lit dew drops, leaving a sparkling trail in our wake. My trainers are wet and so are my feet. They squelch with each step and my thoughts, which until now have meandered contentedly, fixing on nothing in particular, come sharply into focus. Breakfast.

When I lived in a city, before I had livestock or dogs to tend to first thing in the morning, breakfast, more often than not, was either eaten in a rush, standing up in the kitchen, whilst gathering the stuff I needed for the day, or even worse, I'd leave the house, locking the door, with a piece of toast clamped between my teeth and would eat it as I raced along the pavement. And there were plenty of mornings when I didn't bother with breakfast at all. But now it is my most important and, I think, favourite meal of the day. I suspect it is because, having spent an hour or so after getting up feeding and checking my livestock and taking the dogs for a walk or run, I am properly hungry.

As a child I'd always get up early and climb over the fence of the farm next door to help muck out and feed their horses. It was physical work – loading muck into barrows, sweeping, carrying hay, straw and water buckets – and there were a lot of horses to feed and stables to clean. Once these jobs were done, the horses fed and turned out into the fields, we would gather in the farmhouse kitchen, bringing with us the potent fragrance of the stable yard and rumbling tummies. We'd sit at the table with its oilcloth, nursing big mugs of instant coffee made not with water but with milk, and pass around a packet of digestives. Oh, the luxury of wrapping cold hands around a warm mug of steaming, milky coffee and the delicious decadence of a dunked digestive. The final satisfaction of draining the mug and scooping out, with a none-too-clean finger, the remnants of the biscuits that had been dunked that little bit too long. The pleasure of satiation. It was the breakfast of kings. Nothing could beat it.

But now, much as I still love a dunked digestive, it is not thoughts of biscuits and instant coffee that are fuelling me on the final stretch of the morning's run. When we moved to the Welsh countryside from London, the couple we bought our house from asked if we would look after their chickens for a few weeks until they got settled into their new place. I had never looked after chickens before but was only too happy to take on a duty that felt like an initiation into the new way of life I had craved for so long. There were three hens – a big, feathery, chestnut one, a pretty black and white one, and one with speckled plumage and a rather wilful nature. They were called things like Linda and Barbara because their owner had named them after her colleagues at work. There was a cockerel too, very handsome, all comb and tail feathers. I forget his name, but it might have been Bernard. They lived in a wooden coop in the field adjoining the garden and on our first, bitterly cold morning, I crunched through the frost to let them out. The cockerel came out first, beady-eyed and alert, high-stepping over the frozen grass. His harem followed in a carefree gaggle, making straight for the feeder. I filled it with grain and they piled in, clucking and pecking and scattering bits of corn. Their water was frozen solid, so I refilled it from the hot tap in the kitchen and then stood and watched them for a bit.

Chicken-watching, I discovered that day, is strangely captivating. The things they do, the ways they interact, the pecking order, the personalities. Staggering amounts of time can pass, with no sensation of it passing. It was only the cold on this particular morning that eventually roused me from my chicken-watching reverie. Their owners had told me not to expect many eggs, as hens tend not to lay much during the short, dark days of winter, but I checked the house just in case. And there, in the corner, was a single brown egg. I picked it up with the reverence of a treasure hunter, held its smooth warmth carefully in my chilly palm, carried it back to the kitchen with a feeling of something like triumph. It was beautiful. But then eggs are. The simple economy of them. The shape, texture, feel, colour.

We had a thick hedge that grew against the wall outside the kitchen of my childhood home. In spring it flowered, a mass of dark pink blooms that were abuzz with bees. It was a favourite hedge for nesting blackbirds, and I remember my dad lifting me up to look into a nest that was tucked in amongst the twigs, partially hidden by a screen of leaves and flowers. It was a perfect bowl of dried grass and within its protective walls lay four blue-green speckled eggs. I can still remember the sense of wonder at the sight of them and the excitement of finding a jagged-edged fragment on the ground once the chicks had hatched, which I kept for years in a matchbox lined with cotton wool: my own precious jewel.

Of course, I had eaten eggs before. A boiled egg with soldiers was pretty much a staple when I was growing up, but there was something about the egg I collected our first morning in our new home that set it apart. When I sliced off the top, dipped in the spoon, the yolk that spilled over the side was a golden, vibrant yellow, rare in shop-bought eggs, even free-range ones. But it was the taste, the creamy richness of it. That and maybe the fact that I had fed the hen that had laid it. Collected the egg and carried it back to the kitchen to cook. I knew its provenance. I had a connection with it, and I ate it with a sense of appreciation that I had never had before.

Eventually the hens were reclaimed by their owners, packed into cardboard boxes with much affronted clucking and squawks of protest from the cockerel, and driven away in the boot of their car. I missed them and the morning routine that went with them. And I missed that little frisson of pleasure every time I found eggs in the nest box. So we got our own hens, and now can't quite imagine living without them. And as we had the space and a pond, we got some ducks too. Duck eggs were a revelation. Bigger than hens' eggs, the shell has a different texture that is almost porcelain-like and has the almost translucent opaqueness of porcelain too. It's thicker, harder to crack but once opened it reveals an egg that is practically all yolk. Poached and placed with due ceremony on a slice of brown toast, there is no better breakfast. Sometimes I add Marmite to the toast and chilli flakes to the top of the egg, but that's just me and my fancy ways. Unadorned apart from a little salt and pepper, it is simple perfection. I can run for miles if I know there is a poached duck egg as a reward at the end.

*

I'm eating banana bread in Kathy's kitchen. It's a recipe she's been testing and I'm her guinea-pig.

'It's sugar free,' she tells me.

'Don't care,' I say, with my mouth full, 'it's delicious.'

She has toasted it and it's warm and fragrant. She eats hers with butter and honey. I leave mine unadorned.

'Am I allowed the recipe?' I ask, licking the last crumbs off my fingers.

'Of course! I'll send it to you.'

And she did. It's too good not to share, so here is Kathy Slack's recipe for sugar-free, guilt-free, utterly delicious banana bread. Toast it or not, butter or no butter, but I urge you to make it.

Kathy's No-sugar Banana Bread

MAKES 1 LOAF

160g wholemeal flour

80g self-raising flour

1 tsp bicarbonate of soda

1 tsp baking powder

2 tsp ground cinnamon (optional)

300g mashed, overripe banana

4 tbsp runny honey

3 large eggs, beaten

150ml plain yoghurt

Preheat the oven to 160°C.

Mix the flours, bicarbonate of soda, baking powder and cinnamon (if using) in a bowl.

Add all the other ingredients and stir vigorously to make a batter.

Pour into a lined 2lb loaf tin and bake for 1 hour 10 minutes, or until
a skewer comes out clean.
Let it cool (if you can wait that long) before slicing.

*

I haven't come here just to eat – although I manage to do quite a lot of
that (more recipes to follow). I've come here because Kathy writes a
blog I've been reading for a while. It's called *Gluts and Gluttony* and
in it she shares tales and tips from her vegetable garden and recipes
for using up the gluts of vegetables. As anyone who grows vegetables
knows, you can sometimes end up eating an awful lot of one thing until
the very sight of a courgette/beetroot/leaf of rainbow chard makes you
feel slightly nauseous.

Not that this is a problem I face this year. My dream of not having
to buy vegetables for the whole summer quickly faded as crop after
crop failed. I pulled up a grand total of two carrots, no beetroot and
the sprouting broccoli, which started with such promise, came to
little more than a few clumps of pretty green leaves. The lettuce in its
clever guttering beds all died because the soil dried out instantly. The
radishes – my homage to Ottolenghi – grew fabulously bushy, healthy-
looking leaves but when I went, all eagerness, to pull one up there was
nothing beneath the soil apart from a thin, anaemic-looking root.
I pulled up another one. It was the same.

'It's your soil, I'm afraid,' said Emma.

Our soil is heavy clay, as well as being full of stones. When we re-
configured the vegetable beds, made them smaller and higher, we
should, I now realize, have brought in some new topsoil to mix with
our garden compost and some mulch. But we didn't. Soil was soil, as

far as I was concerned. We just refilled the beds with the old stuff from the garden. A lesson learned.

And then there were all those lovely tomato varieties I had chosen with such care and helped plant with such anticipation. The seeds germinated – between us, Emma and I had so many plants we lost count of how many we gave away – but this early success was short-lived. The plants that went outside against the south-facing wall, beautifully protected from the wind, to all intents and purposes drowned, because it rained so much in the early part of the summer and the ones in the greenhouse got too much heat and not enough water. The black ones, which we had both been so excited about, were, in Emma's view, 'universally rubbish', and I couldn't disagree. They produced small black fruits as hard and unyielding as squash balls, but not as big, and never got any softer.

'Tomatoes are high-maintenance plants,' Emma said ruefully. 'They need regular watering, not loads once in a while and then nothing for a week. It's the same for all the veg, really. Working away over the summer as much as you did didn't help. You're going to have to retire.'

The cucamelons produced lots of tendrilly growth that wound its way happily up Paul's hazel sticks, but not a single fruit. We discovered later that we should have pinched out the main shoot when it reached a height of 2.5 metres and the side shoots at 40 centimetres. 'Oops,' said Emma. Emma and Paul both enjoyed the cricket-ball-sized crystal lemon cucumbers, but I thought they were rather underwhelming.

The artichokes, and the promise of a romantic night in with Ludo, dripping lemon butter down our chins, never materialized, and the two varieties of aubergine I tried both failed. Emma blames the chillies and says the sheer number of them cast too much shade in the greenhouse for the aubergines to stand a chance. The dwarf aubergines she grew in her own greenhouse were enormously productive – 'And they were bloody delicious,' she says, smugly. She urges me to try them again next year 'in a world with less chillies'.

Thankfully we did have bumper crops of the dwarf broad beans, which were as vibrant and tasty as they should be, as were the lovely purple French beans (although it is such a shame they don't keep their colour when cooked). The peas, too, were a success, and Emma and I agreed we should have given them more room (rather than that stupid cucamelon, for one thing, observed Emma) so we could have planted more. As it was, I don't think any of the peas ever made it from the vegetable patch because, in honour of Stan, I ate them all in situ.

The chillies, though, much to Emma's chagrin (and to the detriment of the aubergines) absolutely thrived. One entire shelf of the greenhouse is packed with leafy, lustrous plants. Every one of them flowered and many are already wilting under the weight of the fruits. Emma had questioned whether I really did want to grow that many – 'That's a lot of chillies,' she said, in her 'far-be-it-from-me' tone of voice, as I added another variety to the list.

'But I eat them every day,' I said. And I do. Chillies with eggs is one of the finest breakfasts I know. Or lunches. Spiky red chilli with tomatoes, coriander and feta in an omelette. Takes five minutes. Glorious. But, as ever, my dear gardening-guru friend was right and I now have to concede, somewhat ungraciously, that there are probably not enough breakfasts left in my lifetime to eat the number of chillies that are ready to be harvested. I have a glut that even my gluttony can't put a dent in. I've already given some away. I took an entire plant, laden with fruit, to some friends who I was having lunch with. It made them laugh, because their kitchen windowsill was already crowded with highly productive chilli plants of their own. I gave some to my friend Amie to make her wondrously good chilli jam. In return (which seemed a very good trade) I got a jar of the jam and the recipe, so I could make more. If you are ever over-burdened with chillies, this is a very lovely way of using them.

Amie's Chilli Jam

MAKES ABOUT 5 JARS

150g fresh red chilli peppers, deseeded (although I keep some seeds as I like the heat) and chopped

150g red pepper, cored, deseeded and chopped

1kg jam sugar

600ml cider vinegar

Sterilize Kilner jars or old jam jars (I put them on a short hot wash in the dishwasher).

Pulse the chillies and red pepper in a food processor until finely chopped.

Dissolve the sugar and vinegar in a pan over a low heat without stirring.

Add the chilli mixture to the pan and bring to the boil.

Leave at a rollicking boil for 10 minutes.

As the mixture cools, ladle into warm jars.

It can be eaten straight away – it is not one of those preserves that needs to sit for months in a cupboard, by which time you've forgotten you've made it...

*

But still the chillies kept coming and, in need of further inspiration, I got in touch with Kathy, hoping she didn't think it was weird, given that I don't really know her. We had met – very briefly – once or twice at events and knew people in common, which I hoped might be excuse enough. I told her that I had a surfeit of chillies I didn't know what to do with and asked if I could visit her, bringing a bag of them along with me.

What I discovered, while we were munching banana bread and drinking coffee, was how Kathy came to do what she does. I just assumed she was someone who had always cooked, perhaps trained at one of those Cordon Bleu places, and had taken to blogging because that is what so many foodies seem to do these days. But her story is rather more dramatic and a lot more inspiring than that.

One morning she got in the shower and just couldn't work out how to use the mixer tap. It was her shower, one she had used many times, not one of those incomprehensible ones you come across in hotels sometimes that seem to have been specifically designed for maximum confusion and minimum cleanliness. And yet she just looked at this familiar tap and couldn't think how to make it work. Later that morning she got in her car with her key, which she knew she needed to get the car started, she just couldn't remember how or what she needed to do with it. 'I thought I had had a stroke or something.' But that wasn't what had happened.

Now it's worth noting at this point that Kathy Slack is not one of those people you look at with a sad, imperceptible shake of the head and think: *there's a health crisis waiting to happen.* In her early forties, she is the picture of health – slim, fit, shiny-haired, the skin of her unmade-up face clear and glowing. 'Bright-eyed and bushy-tailed' as my mum would put it. Nor has she ever binged on booze, fags and class A drugs – 'I'm too much of a goody two shoes' – which, given the industry she worked in, would have been easy. And pretty normal.

Because after she graduated from university, she got a job as a graduate trainee in an advertising agency. 'I was in my early twenties and it was all quite busy and glamorous and there was a very obvious career ladder that I was determined to climb as quickly as possible. Quite early on, I made the notoriously difficult move from account management to brand strategy. Every couple of years I'd move agency and each time I did, I'd get a big jump in salary. It was pretty silly really, looking back on it now, especially as I'd ended up in advertising more by accident than anything else. But I was earning good money and that is quite addictive.'

In 2014 she was offered a job by 'an amazing agency. They were all lovely and grown-up and smart and everyone was really well looked after. I was on a huge salary – £160,000 or something like that – but I worked every waking hour, often at weekends. I travelled constantly. One month I was in five different continents in four weeks. I had no idea whether I was in Singapore or Delhi and I was permanently jetlagged. This is what I had worked so hard to achieve and yet, I realized, I was miserable. But I felt I'd gone too far down the road to turn back.'

By then she and her husband Paul had moved out of London to the house I've come to today. It's in Oxfordshire, on the edge of the Cotswolds, and they loved the peace and comfort of being in the countryside. Loved being outside in their garden, growing a few vegetables. It was the perfect antidote to Kathy's frenetic work life.

'I don't think I was aware of it at the time, but despite not being happy,

I was hooked on making it to the next level, earning more and more money, even though I didn't need any more. We never took extravagant holidays or went on huge shopping sprees – we didn't have the time. The money was a reflection of success. That's why I aspired to earn more of it. So I carried on – persuading people to buy cheap chocolate that they didn't need and probably couldn't afford, while at home I was buying organic, unprocessed, sugar-free blah de blah and feeling like a complete hypocrite.'

And then the day came when she couldn't turn on the tap in the shower or start her car, when she was, in her words, completely dysfunctional and very scared. She'd suffered a huge mental breakdown. Extreme depression had caused her brain to shut down.

'And yet there was nothing wrong with my life. I wasn't dealing with any sort of trauma, I had everything I could possibly want and people I loved who loved me. But in a way that made the whole thing worse, because I kept thinking: *what on earth have you got to be upset about?*'

Her bosses were enormously understanding and supportive – 'textbook brilliant'. She saw a doctor who signed her off work. Extreme stress had caused a huge chemical imbalance and the only way to right it was to stop working.

'And I told the doctor I couldn't not work. I had workshops to give and presentations to write and she said, "None of this matters." But it did to me. It was my life. Everything was work. There wasn't anything else. It wasn't a healthy way to live, but I'd lost all perspective and, although the breakdown was awful and I wouldn't wish it on anyone, it got me out of a situation I could see no way out of. It was just a pretty drastic way of doing it.'

Her treatment was a combination of drugs, therapy and acupuncture.

She went on holiday, exercised carefully, practised mindfulness with the help of an app called Headspace, which an old colleague of hers who had also suffered from mental illness had developed. She and Paul got a dog, a very sweet spaniel called Hadleigh who is sitting in the kitchen with us now and looks at Kathy constantly with unabashed adoration.

'I tried everything I could think of, even things I was cynical about, and about four months later thought I was probably well enough to return to work. I wasn't. It was a disaster. Within just a week I was pretty much back to square one. And that's when I had to concede that I simply couldn't go back to that job. The train I was travelling on was about to hit a brick wall and I had to get off. I didn't know what I was going to do next, at that point I didn't care, I just knew I had to stop. I had no choice.'

In one UK study, 19 per cent of adults polled said they were unhappy in their jobs but were scared to do anything about it. Many of us feel unable to make the changes that we'd like in our working lives because our jobs define us, give structure and purpose to our lives as well as that all-important salary. People who are unemployed often suffer from low self-esteem, not only because they lack these things in their lives, but also because they feel – and frequently are – judged by those who have work and can't quite imagine life without it.

Kathy acknowledges that although she was, in some ways, miserable doing her job and had lost belief in what she was doing, she would have found it almost impossible to give it up if she hadn't become so ill.

'In one respect I was lucky because that very difficult decision, even though it was absolutely the right one, was taken out of my hands.' But her working life *was* her life, it had dominated everything. Now, she faced the hard and terrifying prospect of having to create a new life, a new identity, reinvent herself. I'm curious – fascinated – to know how she started that process. 'By the time I was able to function again I was so grateful that I was still here. That I was able to wake up in the morning without feeling like I wanted the world to end and that I still had friends, people who loved me and a roof over my head. And that gave me a real sense of clarity – was something of a revelation in fact. Because that's when I realized that those simple things are the things that are truly important and that nothing else matters. I didn't need another big career that was going to define me. I just wanted to do something I enjoyed and the time I spent tinkering about in my garden was something I really enjoyed. It was also a big contributing factor to my recovery. Being able to grow something – see it go from seed to carrot – feels like a real achievement, makes you feel like you have some purpose in the world.'

Her early attempts weren't always a success, mainly, she laughs, 'because I was clueless and started with things that are quite difficult, like red cabbages and sprouts and cauliflowers. I even tried to grow a melon without a greenhouse. Madness! But it didn't matter because, while I was recuperating, just being outside and being reminded that the sun was still coming up, the world was still turning and nature was carrying on doing her thing, was more important. And I just learned by trying things out and didn't worry whether they worked or not.'

It seems slightly audacious that someone with so little gardening experience could think about it as a next career, but recovery made her braver too, less shy and worried about rejection. So she just emailed people she thought she would like to work for, feeling that if they said no, it wasn't a big deal. One of those people was a man called Jez who ran the kitchen garden on a nearby organic farm, supplying the shop, café and cookery school on site.

'I said to him, "I want to grow vegetables for a living but I don't know how, so can I come and work for you?" And it was the summer, and he was really busy, so he said yes. I learned so much and became even more addicted!' And then a permanent job came up at the cookery school. Jez put her forward for it and she got it.

How, though, I wonder, did someone used to a six-figure salary cope with one that I presumed was significantly smaller?

'Ninety per cent smaller!' she laughed. 'Well, to be honest, I probably couldn't have managed if Paul wasn't working full time and also I did have money saved from all those years of working my socks off. But it helped me make the really important discovery that the definition of success is not linked to what you earn, which was absolutely what I believed when I worked in advertising. I had discovered the truth: the real definition of success is doing something you enjoy.'

While talking, Kathy has been stirring a pan of soup on the stove.

'Do you like celeriac?'

I nod.

'Love it!'

'My crop did really well this year, so it's been a bit of a feature of my blog recently.' She pours creamy ladlefuls into bowls, the smell making my stomach growl in happy anticipation. She scatters the surface with small chunks of chopped apple, thyme leaves and a twist of black pepper and hands me a slice from the sourdough loaf she had baked before I arrived. Once again, I begged her for the recipe. Her transformation of an ugly root vegetable into a dish of such beauty demands repeating.

Kathy's Celeriac Soup with Apple and Thyme

SERVES 2

25g butter
half a large celeriac
300ml whole milk

2 tsp thyme leaves, chopped, plus
extra to serve
half an apple, diced ·
salt and pepper

Melt the butter gently in a heavy saucepan while you peel and finely
slice the celeriac. Add it to the butter with a pinch of salt and sweat for
10–15 minutes until the celeriac is very soft. DON'T RUSH THIS!! It
needs to be meltingly soft.

Add half the milk, briefly bring to the boil, then blend with a handheld
whizzer.

Add the thyme.

Over a low heat, gradually add more milk until you have a smooth,
thick soup. Check the seasoning and adjust as you like.

Pour soup into warm bowls and top with diced apple, thyme leaves and
a grind of pepper.

*

Kathy stayed at the cookery school for three years, and it was there
that she started writing about the things she was cooking from the veg
patch and what she was making when there was a three-kilo glut of
beetroot. The notes became a blog and the blog led to her being asked
to cook for private clients. Eventually she became too busy to manage
both jobs. She left the cookery school and set up her own business,
something she never dreamed of doing 'but it sort of set itself up'.

'Can you monetize a blog?' I ask. I'm hopelessly ignorant of these things.

'You can, but I don't. I write it for the pleasure of it. I still cook for private clients. I do a monthly supper club, which I love, and work with a couple of brands developing recipes for them. I'm also doing more writing – I have a regular column in a magazine and contribute to other magazines and websites. But the thing that underpins all this, and that started it all in the first place, is my veg patch.'

'Can we go and see it?'

'Of course! It's across the road.'

Kathy's own garden is big enough to have a couple of raised beds, but she does most of her growing in a large plot belonging to her neighbour.

'It was too much for him to manage, so he suggested I share it. It's a perfect arrangement.'

We walk through the gate and around a hedge into the garden of the house opposite. It is a big space, maybe quarter of an acre, and Kathy has been given about two-thirds of it. It is coming to the end of the growing season now, she points out, so it's looking a bit tatty. But it still has that special allure. There is something so aesthetically pleasing about vegetable beds. They have the same visual interest – all the colour, variety of shape, size and texture – of a border of shrubs and flowers, but perhaps it is the order of them that appeals so much to me. The patchwork-quilt quality: order without uniformity.

I have a nostalgic type of love for patchwork quilts and I'm not sure where it comes from. Hand-made from scrap material, they are practical, comforting and beautiful; the embodiment of perfect simplicity. I have a feeling my grandmother had one, but I honestly can't remember. I like those blankets knitted from different squares too.

When I was growing up, John and Joy, who lived in the house on the other side of the lane from us, used to invite us to come and pick vegetables from their garden. The whole garden was testament to their devotion to it. It was large, and had a big tree in the middle of the lawn, with a swing hanging from its branches. Surrounding the lawn were wonderfully jungly beds, alive with the buzz of bees and the lazy flit of butterflies. But the big square of earth given over to vegetables at the side of the house was my favourite bit. To a young, curious mind, seeing something that is familiar, like a carrot or a radish, appearing from the depths of the dark, crumbly soil when you pull on a sprig of leaves is like a magic trick. I'll never forget the sense of wonder I felt when John dug a fork into a ridge of raised earth and revealed the potatoes it was nurturing. The excitement of kneeling in the earth and digging my hands into it to find these hidden treasures, which we'd take home and bake until their skins were crispy and the insides fluffy and soft.

Kathy and I wander between the rows of cabbages, chard and kale, and pick some of the last of the summer raspberries. She shows me some of the more exotic crops she's tried – her cucamelons have been rather more successful than mine, and what I thought was a sort of pea is actually achocha. It's a relative of the courgette that grows in the High Andes, but seems equally happy in Oxfordshire.

'It's gone a bit rampant,' says Kathy, finding and picking off one of the little green pods from amongst the mass of leaves clambering happily up a fence. She hands me one of the pods to try. It is crispy and watery and sweet, a bit like a cucumber. 'If you fry them, they have this lovely, intense flavour like roasted green peppers and they are so easy to grow.' I put them on my mental list to try next year – my resolution to avoid the exotic already forgotten.

In amongst the vegetables there are marigolds and nasturtiums for companion planting. The nasturtiums are supposed to prevent white fly on cucumbers and tomatoes (and actually, although my tomatoes battled with almost everything that can beleaguer a tomato, white fly wasn't among them, so maybe I can thank my nasturtiums). Marigolds attract insects like ladybirds, lacewings and hoverflies that prey on aphids. Having been so anti-marigold, in light of the fact that mine grew so beautifully when nothing else did, I feel a bit more charitable towards them, and they definitely earn their place in a veg patch. Kathy has also grown dahlias – she's another recent convert to them – which she cuts to decorate the tables at her supper club. She talks about the sense of connection she gets when she is here, fingers amongst the worms and mud under her nails. Feeling part of the world, but also feeling she'd been able to take back a tiny bit of control over her existence.

'When you've had mental-health problems, which are so much about feeling out of control, coming out here on days when I didn't feel able to even make a cup of tea and seeing things growing that I had planted was really powerful. It felt like a huge achievement. You don't waste anything you've grown yourself because you are so astonished that you've grown it! And it changes the way you cook. If I've come out here on a summer's evening and picked courgettes, that is what is for supper. And I'll eat them raw, drizzled with olive oil, lemon and salt, because that's all they need. They are so fresh. I look at them on the plate and think: *three months ago these were just tiny seeds and now they are my dinner*, and it never ceases to amaze and delight me.'

Back in her kitchen, she takes my chillies, spreads them out on a baking tray and puts them in a hot oven. I toast coriander and cumin seeds in a dry frying pan until their warm, spicy aroma fills the kitchen. When their skins are black and charred, Kathy takes the chillies out of the oven and puts them immediately into a small plastic bag and seals it. 'This steams the skins off, so you can peel them easily.' And sure enough, the skins slip obligingly away from the red, orange and green flesh. She deseeds them, but not completely. 'We'll leave a bit of heat.' I pound my roasted spices in a pestle and mortar and Kathy adds garlic cloves, salt and the chillies and tells me to bash them all together to form a paste.

Simple Pleasure #11

— A PESTLE AND MORTAR —

I'm going to go off on a brief tangent here, just to extoll the virtues of a pestle and mortar, because, to me, these two things are a physical manifestation of utilitarian simplicity. My pestle and mortar live on the kitchen windowsill alongside the radio, bowls of fruit, tomatoes (a tomato should never be in the fridge), lemons and a big wooden tray I found in an African market, on which I keep onions, garlic, ginger and vegetables like squash and sweet potatoes that don't need to take up fridge space. This is the joy of living in an old stone house with walls almost a metre thick. Phone signal is rubbish, but the windowsills are great storage space.

The pestle and mortar were a wedding present and they've been used, if not daily, certainly regularly for the last 28 years. The mortar is a bowl of heavy cream stone, carved so that it is flat-bottomed on the outside, with smooth tactile sides curving upwards and rounding over at the top. That thick, curved top edge forms a perfect circle, interrupted only by a carefully shaped spout. The interior is a half sphere, the cream faintly discoloured and stained, bearing witness to the years of use. The pounding end of the pestle is the same heavy cream stone attached to a pale wooden handle shaped so as to be comfortable to grip and just the right length to accommodate a curled fist. The spare and practical design is timeless, as are the objects themselves. In Southwest Asia, stone mortars and pestles have been found that date back to around 35,000 BC and yet look remarkably like their modern-day counterparts. Using a pestle and mortar has the same primeval quality of any fruitful manual labour. Like kneading or planting or digging. Harder work than getting a machine to do it for you, but the soothing rhythm it forces you to adopt gives the mind a chance to wander. A chance I relish whenever I get it.

*

To my muddle of chillies, garlic and spices, Kathy adds tomato purée, lemon juice, olive oil and a couple of drops of rosewater. She stirs it, scoops a little up with the spoon and hands it to me to taste. 'Harissa,' she says. I close my eyes to appreciate fully the kaleidoscope of flavour; the smoky, spicy heat, the fruity richness of the tomato and the delicate floral notes from the rosewater. And resolve to grow even more chillies next year.

Harissa

MAKES 1 SMALL JAR

12–16 large fresh chilli peppers
(we used a mixture of colours
and varieties)
1 tsp coriander seeds
1 tsp cumin seeds
4 garlic cloves

half a tsp salt
2 tsp tomato purée
juice of half a lemon
1 tbsp olive oil
few drops of rosewater (optional –
but I wouldn't miss it out)

Preheat the oven to 220°C.

Arrange the chillies in a single layer on a baking tray and roast for 20–25 minutes until the skins are charred and black.

Remove from the oven and put them straight into a plastic bag. Seal it and leave for 5 minutes.

Once the chillies are cool enough to handle, peel and deseed them (leaving some seeds if you like heat).

Toast the coriander and cumin seeds in a dry pan, then crush to a powder in a pestle and mortar.

Add the garlic, salt and peeled chillies, and continue to pound until you have a paste. (This doesn't take long – and is infinitely quicker and more pleasurable than washing up a food processor.)

Stir in the tomato purée, lemon juice, olive oil and rosewater (if using).

Store in a jar in the fridge and use within a week. (Very, very delicious on roast chicken, by the way.)

Nurturing Nature

Simple Pleasure #12

— BRAMBLING —

I've been working for the last couple of days in the west of Wales. The drive home is long, but the treat of a summer evening is that it is still light and warm when I get home, the sun spreading its long, golden fingers over the fields. I open the door to the barrage of barking that is the welcome I get from the dogs and persuade them to come and have a leg stretch with me. We walk up the farm lane and take the path that climbs diagonally up our neighbour's field. The far hedge is laden, as it always is at this time of year, with particularly juicy blackberries. I remember coming up here one late-summer weekend when we had friends to stay, to pick blackberries for lunch. In no time at all we had filled a bucket – far too many for the one crumble we had planned. We ended up making several, pressing one on our friends to take home for their freezer, as well as jam. Blackberry jam, with its opulent, jewel-like colour and rich fruitiness, turns a piece of toast into a culinary sensation. Ludo puts it on rice pudding, which he then eats with his eyes closed in a state of bliss. But not even blackberry jam can make rice pudding palatable to me.

I don't know why this hedge should be so, literally, fruitful. I'm on its east-facing side. Our prevailing winds and weather come from the west, so this side is protected, which might have something to do with it. It also gets the full benefit of the morning sun as soon as it rises above the tree-covered ridge of Offa's Dyke opposite. When there are sheep in the field, which is usually around lambing time as it is close to the farmhouse, I've often seen them lying up here along the line of hedge in the early mornings, basking in those first rays of sun.

Mum is coming to stay for the night. I didn't have a chance to shop for anything for supper, so I've had to be inventive. I found a piece of pork in the freezer. There are a couple of sad fennel bulbs in the fridge, but the Bramley tree in the garden already has some ripe apples, so I reckon if I roast apples and fennel together under the pork, the sad state of the fennel will be disguised. There's also plain yoghurt in the fridge and a jar of home-made lemon curd from the local farm shop – all that's needed to make my favourite cheat's pudding. Mix plain yoghurt and lemon curd together (add lemon zest if you have a lemon and you want a bit of extra lemony-ness) and you have an instant sort of lemon mousse. Full credit for this culinary wizardry goes to Elisa Benyon, author of the *Vicar's Wife's Cook Book*. She serves the mousse with blackberries and so shall I.

Plastic bowl in hand, I mooch along the hedge as the dogs scamper and sniff. There are a lot of berries here. I test them with my fingers, only picking the ones that pull away easily. They are irresistible and soon my tongue as well as my fingers are tell-tale purple.

Why is it, I wonder, that the fruit you pick yourself tastes so much better? It's fresh – obviously – not chilled and tasteless, and perhaps, because it takes a bit of effort (although in the case of these blackberries, the effort is minimal) and you consciously choose each fruit you pick, you have a greater appreciation for it, which maybe enhances the experience of eating it.

The parents of a friend of ours in London lived a few miles outside Lyme Regis in Dorset. On one or two weekends every summer, a gang of us would be invited to stay. A tradition quickly developed. We would drive down late on a Friday evening and on Saturday morning would take the road to Lyme Harbour and get on one of the little boats that take tourists out to catch mackerel. We would spend a happy couple of hours puttering along just offshore, trailing our lines and hooks behind the boat until we had a few fish in our buckets. On the way back to the house we'd stop at the local Pick Your Own Fruit farm to gather strawberries, raspberries and currants and return with laden punnets on our laps, trying to resist the lure of their perfumed scent that is so synonymous with summer.

Once at the house, we would sit at a table in the garden, hulling the fruits and mixing them for the giant summer pudding they were destined for. When they were ready, they were tipped into the bread-lined bowl, which was then topped with a plate weighted down with a couple of tins of tomatoes and left in the cool of the pantry. We would lounge in the garden with the papers or walk in the woods, until it was time to light the barbeque and prepare the fish. And then we would feast on food all the more delicious because we had been the ones who had caught it and picked it.

My bowl of blackberries is gradually filling up, despite the fact I'm eating one for every few I pick. Before long it is full. Dogs and I turn back, walk through the warm evening shadows with our wild bounty that costs nothing but will taste better than anything money can buy.

*

OVER THE SEA AND FAR AWAY

*

I feed the pigeons. I sometimes feed the sparrows too.
It gives me a sense of enormous wellbeing.
And then I'm happy for the rest of the day, safe in the knowledge
that there will always be a bit of my heart devoted to it.

BLUR, 'PARKLIFE'

I spend the night in my camper van in a field just inland from the North Devon coast. I wake up early and, as there are a couple of hours before I have to catch the boat, I park at the harbour and go for a walk. It is a morning to be celebrated outdoors, in the salty sea air and the warm luxury of the sun.

I know there are people who, as soon as they wake up, reach for their phones and check their social media. This is not how I want my first waking view of the world to be dictated. I don't want my state of mind to be influenced by what other people are doing or saying or feeling. I know it is infuriating when someone forms an intractable, negative opinion of something they have never tried or used, and I am guilty of doing that very thing. Because that is how I feel about Facebook. I've never used it, never been on it and nor do I have the slightest wish to. I don't want to hear news of the people I love and care about that way.

I remember, all too vividly, receiving the phone call to tell me that Mike, a colleague and dear friend, had been killed. Moments later, my phone rang again. Mike's many friends were ringing around, not just to share the news, but to ensure that everyone who needed to be aware of this awful tragedy had been told. Between us, we made lists of people to contact and continued the sad task of spreading the news of our friend's death. Barely half an hour after I'd first heard, I phoned someone who both Mike and I had worked with over the years, and before I said anything, he said, 'You're phoning about Mike.' 'Yes,' I said, 'someone already called you?' 'No. It's on Facebook.'

I can't imagine how I would have felt if I had got news of Mike's death that way. It seems such a detached, impersonal way to discover something so affecting. And so lonely. I needed to hear the voices of Jo and Keith, Lucy and Simon, hear their shock and grief that mirrored mine. I needed to talk about Mike, to laugh about him: how preposterous he could be, how demanding. How he embraced everything, every part of his life, with great gusto and enthusiasm and quite a lot of noise. How sensitive and kind and daft and funny he was. What a hole he had left behind in all our lives.

Some of the pivotal moments of my career were with Mike, life-changing encounters and experiences. The first time we worked together was in the Cayman Islands, trying to capture on film a rarely seen, little-known species of shark. It was a big break for me and a hugely important assignment. This particular shark lives in very deep water, too deep to dive, so we were going to film it from a submarine. Unsurprisingly, I had never been in a submarine before and I was not at all sure how I was going to cope with being sealed up in a very small space with 300 metres of water above my head. And I was already nervous because I knew what an extraordinary opportunity I had been given and I was terrified of messing up.

Mike knew I was scared but was kind enough not to say anything. Kinder still, he found ways of keeping me busy, of distracting me, of making me laugh. The encounter we eventually had with the shark is one I will never forget. It inspired in me a whole new wonder and delight in the natural world. Some years later, it was Mike who helped me through another experience, just as memorable but for different reasons. We were filming in a remote part of the Pacific. Mike wanted to get shots of a shipwreck at night and I went as his lighting assistant. The dive was relatively deep – 30 metres or so – but the conditions were perfect: warm water and no current. Just as we were finishing up, my regulator (the bit of kit you breathe through) failed and my mask flooded with water. Not able to breathe or see, 30 metres down and in the dark, this was not a great situation to be in. But in an instant Mike spotted what had happened. He took my arm in a reassuring grip, gave me his spare regulator so I could breathe again, then guided me slowly to the surface.

'Jesus, Humble!' he shouted, spitting out his regulator as we bobbed about waiting for the boat to come and pick us up. 'Don't do that again! You nearly gave me a heart attack!' And he laughed his big, raucous laugh. Then, suddenly sincere, he said, 'Well done for not panicking. Good job.'

'Oh, I was panicking,' I said, jocularly, 'I'm just very good at hiding it.' But I wasn't being entirely truthful. Because actually I hadn't panicked. I was scared. Very scared. But Mike was there, and I knew he'd keep me safe.

So I don't start my day scrolling through social media. I don't care what people are wearing, what they are having for breakfast, or how many pull-ups they've done in the gym. And if that makes me out of touch and out of the loop, so be it. Because what matters to me is what is going on in the real, visceral, unfiltered world on my doorstep. And the best way to find out is by walking.

I walk around the small harbour and up the road on the other side. There's a steep, grassy headland that I imagine, if I can get to it, will give far-reaching views over the town and out across the sea. I find the path and follow it, brambles giving way to gorse as I gain height. I reach one viewpoint, but the path carries on up the hill and so do I, enjoying the feeling of muscles being stretched and breathing in the energizing air that comes in off the sea, carried by a playful breeze. When I reach the top, the harbour and town are so far below they look like a scene from a model village. There was a model village near my grandparents' house. It still exists today. I loved going there. The feeling of being in another world, as if I'd followed the white rabbit down a hole and emerged in a miniature wonderland. I stand on the edge of the cliff, taking in the silence, watching the wheeling acrobatics of the gulls above the wake of a small boat making its way out to sea.

I choose another path to take a different route back, pause to pat a dog and exchange 'good mornings' with its owner. Back at my van, I put the kettle on, make a mug of tea and sit with it on a bench at the harbour's edge. The town is starting to wake up now. Delivery vans, dog walkers, the shutters going up on the newsagents. Cars pull up alongside mine in the car park and people start to queue outside the ticket office, waiting for it to open. There are families in bright holiday clothes, clutching beach bags, couples in walking boots with rucksacks and caps. And then a tall, slim man, with unruly dark hair, the beginnings of a beard, glasses and a big, friendly smile comes over and says hello. This is Dean, warden of the Island of Lundy, and the man I've come to see. He introduces me to his girlfriend, Zoe. They've both been off the island for a few days to go to a friend's wedding. The crowd at the harbour edge starts to shuffle forward. The boat is ready to go. They shoulder their rucksacks and, once all the passengers have boarded, we get on too and head to the bridge.

Lundy is a small island in the Bristol Channel, a couple of hours by boat from Ilfracombe. I've dived around its shores – it was the UK's first Marine Nature Reserve – but I've never been on the island itself. Despite its remoteness, and the fact that it is surrounded by steep cliffs with no easy place to land a boat, the island has been inhabited for over 3,000 years. The name is attributed to the Vikings and means Puffin Island. It has had a fairly turbulent history, involving pirates, disgraced nobility and smugglers, and has been bought and sold a number of times. The last private family to own it sold it in 1968. It was bought by the National Trust and is leased by the Landmark Trust, which took on the responsibility for restoring, maintaining and running the island. The 23 buildings that make up the only village can be rented out for holidays, and Dean and his conservation team look after the island's wild habitat and introduce visitors to its rich and varied wildlife.

I'd forgotten that the Bristol Channel can be notoriously bumpy. Even today, when the sun is out and there is only the lightest breeze, there is a swell, which I don't notice until I start to get that all-too-familiar feeling that tells me I need to curl up on the floor and pray for land. Zoe, Dean and I are standing at the bow of the boat, drinking coffee with the captain. Mildly embarrassed, I ask if I can go and lie on the floor of his little office behind the bridge. 'You can have a bunk, if you like!' he says, kindly. I apologize to my hosts and disappear, cursing my useless sea-legs.

'We're almost there,' Dean tells me, popping his head around the door. 'You OK?' And I'm fine. I've never understood why anyone thinks looking at the horizon is a cure for seasickness. It just makes me feel sicker. Lying down requires no need for balance; I can shut my eyes and pretend I'm not at sea at all. Works every time.

Back outside, I expect to see dramatic, rocky cliffs rising up out of the sea, but all is obscured by a thick blanket of grey fog.

'Where did that come from?' I ask, amazed. 'The skies couldn't have been clearer when we left the shore.'

'It's often like this. It'll burn off soon enough.' And by the time we've walked up the steep road to the village, and Dean has gone to dump his bag and pick up the Land Rover, the fog has lifted completely.

'Oh, it's going to be beautiful out there,' says Dean, happily. 'I've only been away for a few days, but I really miss it when I'm not here.'

I jump into the passenger seat beside him and we bump and sway our way along the dirt road towards the island's far southern tip.

Dean was born in Northern Ireland, growing up on the Antrim coast. His father, a keen birdwatcher, would take him to Rathlin Island, where they would wild camp and Dean would 'just follow him around with a pair of binoculars'. Those early years and the time he spent on the rugged clifftops of Rathlin with his dad, and the sights, sounds and smells of tens of thousands of seabirds that breed there, were truly formative. Aged ten, he told his dad that he would one day be a marine biologist. But when he reached university age he had a crisis of confidence, didn't believe he had the necessary academic acumen to follow his dream. And not growing up in a wealthy family, he felt he should aim for a career that offered the chance of a good salary. So he studied engineering. And excelled at it, 'but I knew in my heart that that was not what I was supposed to be doing. The books I was reading for pleasure were bird books and books on marine biology. So I bit the bullet, enquired if I could change degree and ended up in

Edinburgh studying marine biology.' But unlike many of his fellow students, Dean's fascination was not what went on beneath the surface of the sea, but above it – the shore birds and the seabirds that had so captivated him as a child. His lecturers were hugely supportive, helped him get the volunteer placements that are so crucial as a first step in a career in conservation. And when he completed his degree he knew not only that he wanted to work on seabird colonies, but that he wanted to be based on an island.

'Wildlife and nature are my impetus to do almost everything. And I knew I would experience nature much more closely in the wild, remote setting of an island, rather than on the mainland. And the time I spent with my dad on Rathlin taught me, really early on, that being on an island with a seabird colony is where I find excitement, but also peace and tranquillity.'

Seabird colonies are not generally associated with peace and tranquillity. They are noisy, smelly, frenetic places, but they are, nonetheless, captivating. In common with human communities, there is always something going on – a domestic drama, a love story, a birth, a death. There's crime and punishment, courtship, acceptance and rejection. There are heart-warming reunions between birds that pair for life, and heartbreak when a partner fails to return. A seabird colony is a soap opera, with a cast of many thousands.

I'm here too late in the year to witness the full majesty of the colonies that nest on the west and south sides of Lundy. From March to July, the cliffs Dean and I are walking towards will be teeming with birds, but now it's the end of the breeding season, the chicks have fledged and the adults leave the colony to moult. So I ask Dean to describe what it is like in the height of the season and he gives a huge, ecstatic sigh of pleasure.

'It's just completely alive, particularly at that point there. That's Jenny's Cove. There might be a few puffins and fulmars hanging around there now, but during the season there will be thousands of guillemots. Thousands of them. And you walk over the brow as we've just done and you smell the colony first, then you hear it and then, just as you come over this last rise, you see a sea of black and white and red bills, with gulls circling overhead creating havoc.'

Part of Dean's job here on Lundy is to monitor the seabird populations and, in the breeding season, he will come here every day and sit for at least two to three hours watching puffins or guillemots in the morning, and then another two to three hours watching kittiwakes and fulmars in the afternoon. For many, the thought of sitting on a cliff in possibly – probably – not the most clement weather (Lundy is very exposed), watching distant black-and-white birds on ledges for hours at a time, is not overly appealing. I wonder what it is that makes it so compelling for Dean. Part of it, he tells me, is he knows how important it is to learn from these birds. They are really good environmental indicators, can tell us so much about the health of our seas and oceans. Monitoring them, says Dean, gives tremendous insight into what is going on out at sea. And even though he has been working with seabird colonies on various islands now for many years (Lundy is his fifth island home), he still gets a great rush of excitement when the first birds return.

'And then afterwards, when I'm with them every day, it is a place I feel relaxed. I settle in with my telescope for a couple of hours, watch the birds feeding their chicks, and that for me is the best therapy, just watching that. In one sense I feel really small, seeing all those birds just going about their normal lives, uninterested and unaffected by me. But it also makes me feel special, that I have the privilege to witness this time in their life histories, gain some insight into their lives, before they disappear again.'

I'm surprised he uses the word 'therapy', only because Dean appears to be so well-adjusted and content.

'I am content, very much so, but it is because I spend my time outside with nature. I know what I can be like when I have long periods away from it. I crave it, in a sense. It is such a part of me. When I'm closed off from it, I feel an itch. I know when the bird migration is kicking off, or when there is the best chance of seeing a rare bird and I feel an urgent need to be there and I feel really unhappy if I'm not.'

Island life suits him too. Lundy is small – just 3 miles long and half a mile wide and Dean is one of a population of just 28 who live here all year round. They are, Dean says, 'like one huge family. There's a nice mix of ages and we're all very sociable. Even when we're not working, we hang out together. We're all quite like-minded. It's the island, and our shared love of it, its wildness and its wildlife that brings us together. I've made friends here that will be friends for life.'

Lundy has one small shop and one pub. There's limited internet and no mobile phone signal, but nature provides the entertainment. They go snorkelling and kayaking, swim at night in a sea glowing with bioluminescence, watch meteor showers. Or sometimes they just lie in the sun with a drink and talk. Many of the visitors who come over on day trips or to stay in one of the cottages find it hard to fathom how anyone can live like this, but, Dean says, 'It is exciting, spontaneous, wild. No two days are the same. There's always something different going on. I love that. And of course the wildlife is spectacular.'

Island life is not without its challenges though. As Dean describes it, 'It is a simple life that can sometimes be really complicated.' Electricity, is, at the moment, supplied by diesel generators, although the plan is to switch to renewable energy in the near future. Last year, when the island was hit by a violent snowstorm, they had no electricity for three days. And there is no mains water on the island either. The people living here, the farm livestock and all the visitors rely on rainwater that is collected and stored in big tanks. And when they have a drought year, which happens more often than you might expect on an island in the middle of the Bristol Channel, they have to restrict their water use dramatically. That means no showers, for sometimes days or even weeks; no flushing loos. In severe drought years, a boat has had to bring water from the mainland.

Food also has to come in by boat or by helicopter, but neither can get to the island if the weather is too bad. There are allotments, so they can grow a certain amount of vegetables, and the island has its own small abattoir, so the livestock that helps manage the habitat for wildlife also helps feed the islanders. But everything else has to be brought in. The little shop sells essentials like bread, milk, tea and coffee.

'And snacks! It is always really exciting when something new comes over. The other day we got Magnum ice creams with cookie bits in them. We'd never had those before and everyone on the island just had to have one. They were cleared out in two hours!'

The island's isolation is never more apparent than when something breaks down. Getting an engineer to come out, getting spare parts, all takes a lot longer and costs a lot more than it would on the mainland. So, as Dean puts it, 'We have to go back to the old way of doing things. We can't have the throwaway attitude that so many people have. We have to fix things as best we can. We have to make do.'

But the complications are part of the enjoyment of living this way too.

'People living on the mainland take water, electricity, working vehicles for granted. If your car breaks down, you get someone to fix it. If something breaks, you can just throw it away and replace it. Everything is easy. Living here makes you really appreciate having those simple, basic things. It also reminds you that so many people in the world don't have them – don't have access to electricity or water – and you realize how lucky we are.'

'Do you ever hanker after a more "normal" way of life?' I ask, although I'm pretty sure I know what he'll say. There are few people I've met of his age (he's in his early thirties) – of any age, in fact – who are as self-aware and comfortable in their own skin, who have identified what makes them content and have found a way of life that underpins that contentment.

'The core thing for me, the thing that makes me truly happy, is feeling close to nature, feeling a connection with it. And the way you live on a small island like this is dictated by nature on a daily basis. I think that's what makes me feel so rooted here. So much part of it. I was so lucky that my dad taught me this love of nature and that both my parents encouraged me to get out into the wilds and do what makes me happy. You don't have to live the way society prescribes, but unfortunately we are not taught that in school. I started out doing engineering because I thought that was a way to make money and money was what we need to live good, happy lives. But we don't. The only thing I miss living this way is my family, of course. And take outs! Every now and then I do have a craving for a curry!'

Simple Pleasure #13

— A MURMURATION —

It is a truly horrible afternoon. The storm that has been raging for the last 24 hours is showing no sign of abating. Brutal gusts of wind roar around the house and drive the rain against the windows so hard it sounds like someone throwing gravel. But the dog needs a walk and so do I. I'm in hill country but this is not the weather to be out in the hills. The visibility is so bad that the peaks I can usually see from my window have been rendered invisible by the drenching cloud that reaches to the ground. Everything is grey and sodden. So instead I make for flatter land. The map tells me that not far from here there is parkland criss-crossed with footpaths. Probably not very exciting walking but the weather will provide the excitement.

I park at the side of the lane by a fence. There's a footpath sign and a stone stile that we cross and drop down into the field on the other side. Cattle have been in here recently. Many farmers will bring their cattle into sheds when the winter weather takes hold, to save their ground from getting irreparably churned up. There are no cattle in here now, but what appeared from over the fence to be a field of grass proves to be a miserable expanse of standing water and cloying mud disguised by the clumps of grass that haven't been trampled into the mire. Thankfully our timing seems to have coincided with a pause in the worst fury of the storm, although I fear it is simply drawing breath before the next onslaught. The wind still sweeps across the landscape in occasional violent gusts, but at least, I say to the dog in an effort to find cheer in this cheerless adventure, it's not raining.

Walking is difficult. We slither and squelch until, with some relief, we reach a tarmac drive, which the right of way follows. It comes to a collection of buildings where the path leaves the drive and skirts around them. There doesn't seem to be the grand house that I had imagined, majestically overlooking its parkland, at the end of this long driveway. Instead there is more like a small hamlet of cottages, some clearly lived in – there are cars outside and children's swings in gardens, moving, rather eerily, back and forth by themselves in the wind. But others are in varying states of decay and dereliction and as we continue along the track we pass more buildings, windows broken and roofs collapsing in on themselves. There is something discomforting about the whole place and I'm glad to leave it behind and drop down into a scraggy patch of woodland to follow a muddy path over a stream, now a torrent of grey-brown water threatening to burst its banks.

I emerge through a gate into another soggy field and follow the path along its boundary to a village. Here I have the choice of retracing my steps – which I'm not keen to do – or, by taking a less direct route along a mixture of lanes and footpaths, I can return a different way. I opt for this. It is not a good decision. Clearly, even in more clement conditions, this isn't a way that many – or any – people walk. The paths are frequently choked with brambles or no longer exist: where there is a path marked on the map, on the ground there is a thick, well-established and impenetrable hedge. Even my agile dog is scuppered on occasion and, to get her over the many obstacles she can't jump, squeeze under or find a way around, I have to lift her, transferring the mud caking her undercarriage on to me. And it is now that the storm gets its breath back. The wind redoubles its efforts and the rain returns, pellet-like drops that are driven with stinging force into my cheeks and eyes.

Muddied and less than enchanted by our route, we finally scramble over a gate and onto a quiet road that runs alongside a farmyard. Even though it is still relatively early in the afternoon and the winter days are starting to get incrementally longer, the daylight, which has remained dim and watery since dawn, is giving up and fading to dusk. As we plod along, eyes half-shut against the driving rain, I become aware that the sky is full of the dark silhouettes of hundreds of birds, swirling and swooping, creating endlessly shape-shifting patterns as if I am looking through a kaleidoscope. As I draw closer, I can see that this flock is part of many hundreds more birds that have gathered to roost in the bare, twiggy hawthorns alongside a sileage pit. Even over the noise of the wind, I can hear their cacophonous chatter and the beating of thousands of wings.

I've seen starling murmurations before, over the sea at Aberystwyth as they come in to roost under the pier, and above the reed beds of the Somerset levels. Thousands and thousands of birds in what is one of nature's most spectacular displays. This, in comparison, is a small gathering, but still I am transfixed by its balletic beauty. I forget the rain and the mud and the bramble scratches and stand in the empty road, my spirit soaring alongside the birds.

*

Life
Lessons

AN OBSERVATION

*

Living simply – or trying to live more simply, which is, perhaps, a more honest assessment of what I'm attempting – is, it turns out, not always simple. It involves not just a change in mindset, but a shift in habits and a different use of time. The change in mindset came naturally – I didn't have to force it. The idea of living more simply had real appeal. It felt completely intuitive, a natural next step along life's unpredictable path. It was a solution, an answer, rather than a task to be wrestled with.

What I am wrestling with is fitting it into a life that already has a pattern. Had I started this 12 years ago, when we made a big change to our lives – moved from the city to the countryside; swapped roads, pavements and streetlights for a dirt track, woods and fields; a tiny, urban courtyard garden for a 4-acre smallholding – it might have been easier. But I fear I'm making excuses, because that move did achieve what I longed for it to do. It allowed me to live in a way that feels more connected, more in tune with the natural world. I understand and appreciate the seasons more, enjoy being active witness to the shifts in colour, smell and sound they bring to the world. I start my day not rushing along a pavement to catch the 94 bus, but in wellies, feeding my pigs, checking the sheep, letting out the chickens and ducks and collecting eggs. I walk the dogs, accompanied not by traffic noise and fumes, but by birdsong and in clean, fresh air. And all those things are elements of the simple life I seek. So perhaps the shift towards a life more simple started – without me thinking of it that way – with that move, and what's happening now is a more conscious attempt to take it further. And that's the challenge. Because although we all live differently, the foundations that dictate much about the way we live are very similar for many of us. And the most prevalent and controlling of those foundations is debt.

I'm not talking about credit cards or loans or university debt – something, mercifully, I avoided by being of an age before fees were introduced and choosing not to go anyway. I'm talking about a debt that we actively aspire to have. That has even become a badge of a kind of success. The mortgage. If I was 23 again (the age I was when I got married and together we applied for our first mortgage), there is no way on earth any bank would consider lending us money today. Because both of us were freelance and starting our television careers. My husband, Ludo, eight years my senior, was a bit more established but still had a pretty sporadic income. I was very much at the start, earning practically nothing and living an entirely hand-to-mouth existence. But amazingly we got an £80,000 mortgage with which to buy a small, terraced house in Shepherd's Bush.

Pretty much everything we earned went straight to the building society to pay not the debt, but the interest on the debt. But that didn't matter, because we were on the property ladder and that was an achievement. But the choice we made (and were lucky to be able to make), to buy a house with money we didn't have, took away other choices and other options, because now we were beholden to that debt. It dictated that we would be making monthly payments for at least the next 30 years. And that still means earning enough to make those payments. Now, contrary to what many people think, television is not a career you go into if you want to make money, certainly not in the UK. If we had wanted to earn big bucks, or even just have a level of financial security, we'd have chosen very different careers. We are fortunate to both have jobs we enjoy, but the money we earn is, nonetheless, essential if we are to keep on top of the mortgage. And when the work doesn't come in, we don't enjoy that 'time off', because it isn't time off. It's time we should be working, should be earning, because there is still that debt to pay.

One evening (oh, it was wild!), we sat down with our bank statements and Ludo put together a spreadsheet of what we spend our money on every month. We live a not particularly extravagant existence. Rural living is good for that. Entertainment tends to be with friends, at each other's houses, rather than at bars or restaurants. We go to the theatre or cinema occasionally. Neither of us enjoys shopping for clothes or feels the need to be decked out in designer garb. 'I'm guessing,' I said, as Ludo punched figures into his computer, 'our biggest expenses aside from the mortgage are food and petrol.' 'Pretty much,' he nods. 'But if we didn't have the dogs or the animals or the garden, we'd be millionaires!' And this is the lunacy of the way we live. The mortgage means we have to work to be able to make the monthly payments. When we are working – which often involves being away from home for long hours or sometimes days or weeks – we also need to pay someone to walk the dogs, or house sit, feed the livestock and tend the garden.

If we didn't have the debt, we wouldn't have to work, and we wouldn't have to pay other people to do things for us. Things that we would actually rather enjoy doing ourselves. Not that either of us want to stop working, because we like it. But we would have the freedom to choose when to work. And the time spent not working would be proper 'time off', and we'd be able to enjoy it, be in the garden, or out with the dogs, guilt- and stress-free and not having to pay someone to do those things on our behalf. We would, in fact, find it a lot easier to live more simply. A simple life, I'm beginning to understand, is not one that requires lots of money, but one that is not dictated by debt.

I was mulling this over with my friends Clare and Sam at supper one evening. Whenever I think of these two, I smile. They have a wonderful approach to life, they embrace it, no holds barred. Sam is a scientist, a brilliant and dedicated naturalist, who is never happier than when he is out in a meadow with a butterfly net. Clare is a photographer, but I also think of her as a collector of people – wonderful, diverse people of all ages and walks of life – and she likes nothing better than to get them together, to spark conversation, ideas and friendship. As I sit here now, the table I'm writing at is covered in notebooks, scribbled-on bits of paper, reminders, torn-out articles and printed-off pages. After that evening Clare sent me a torrent of links, ideas, essays and phone numbers, including one that she'd been particularly emphatic I must call. 'You MUST meet Beth and Jo. You will LOVE them. All that stuff we talked about – they've done it.'

I DON'T THINK WE ARE PARTICULARLY EXTRAORDINARY
*

'Look out for the pub on the left,' Beth had said on the phone, 'and just before it on the right is a little lane going off at an angle. Go down there and keep going until you can't go any further. You'll see our van.'

I've turned down a lane that matches Beth's description but still I feel doubtful. It doesn't feel like the lane to a house. The broken tarmac winds beneath a tunnel of straggly vegetation – elders and brambles – and past a derelict-looking workshop with a pile of scrap metal outside. It's narrow. I'm hoping not to meet a dead end because it will be a tricky reverse to get out and there is nowhere to turn around. But I come to an open space, a sort of yard, gravelled, with low brick buildings on one side, a couple of shipping containers, a metal frame of indeterminate purpose and four large rusty storage tanks that look like they might once have held oil. There is also a yellow van, a blue house and an expansive green view over marshland to the distant hazy horizon where sea and sky meet. It's a warm, gusty day, bright sun and blousy clouds. Jo, in white shirt and straw hat, and Beth, in dungarees and sandals, scamper down a flight of metal stairs to meet me.

'What is this place?!' I laugh, as we hug. 'It's – I don't know – rather bizarre and wonderful and totally unexpected.'

'Come and see it,' Beth said, 'and we'll tell you its story.'

We are on the edge of the Loughor Estuary in South Wales, which, because it drains almost entirely at low tide, is, to this day, the site of a thriving cockle industry. But there's coal under our feet and the tumps that surround their house, now covered in trees and bushes and full of wildlife, Beth says, are slag heaps, remains of when the coal was used to smelt copper shipped from Anglesey. The site was commandeered during the Second World War by the Ministry of Defence. Gun barrels were calibrated here, and they would fire high explosive and mustard-gas shells towards the old cast-iron lighthouse way out on the point. Apparently, Jo tells me with a laugh, they had a flag they would raise to let the cockle pickers know when they could go back to the marsh without fear of being blown up! After the war, the buildings became used for manufacturing – at one time it was surgical dressings, and later, miniature bricks for architects' models.

'Really?' I ask, 'Is there, was there, a need for such a business?!'

Jo shrugs.

'Apparently. But from the 1960s it became an oil depot where oil and petrochemicals were stored and distributed.'

Quite a history, but not the sort of land you'd imagine anyone would choose to live on. Unless you are Jo and Beth. It was exactly what they were looking for. It was perfect.

The pair met at art college. Beth grew up in a family of painters and started selling her own paintings from the age of 16. By the time she got to college, she had £20,000 saved. 'We lived so rurally, there was nothing going on, so I had nothing to spend it on.' And Jo, a sculptor and performer, had been left £20,000 by his grandmother when she died. Beth was 20, Jo 22, and they decided they wanted to live together and work together and maybe raise a family. And they had all this money.

'We thought we were absolutely loaded, but we were continuously told that we didn't have enough to buy anywhere outright. It was a nice big deposit for a house. But we looked around at all the people who were taking on mortgages and all the time they spent slaving away to pay them and we realized that what we wanted more than anything was time, and to spend it working on our own things. We didn't want to give our time to someone else just so we could earn money to pay back the bank. So our number-one rule was No Debt. It didn't feel like a radical or alternative idea. It felt like it was the only thing to do.'

Had I had the foresight or the self-awareness of Beth and Jo, and understood the restrictions debt puts on us all, I'm still not sure I would have been brave enough to do what they did. I might have tried living in a commune, shacked up in a yurt or something, but Beth said they had never wanted to live like that – they didn't aspire to *be* alternative or to be cut off from the real world. Their aspirations, she felt, were still conventional; they just wanted to find a different way of achieving them. And the answer was to buy land, but land that wasn't being offered by estate agents.

'Because,' Jo says, 'that land was always beyond our price range. So we tried all different sorts of avenues – cold calling farms, putting up notices in community shops and outside church halls. *Young local couple, land wanted, cash waiting.*'

Beth picks up the story. 'It was Jo who found this site. He'd spotted this building that you can see from the marsh.' The building, which we are in front of now, stands on its own, away from the main site. It looks like a set from *Breaking Bad* – a low-rise mishmash of brick, concrete and chipboard with very dirty, reflective glass doors, two old, long-defunct diesel pumps outside it and tyres on the roof. It has, as far as I can make out, not a single appealing feature and certainly nothing that would make me – or anyone, unless you're Jo – think this could be a potential place to live and bring up children.

'But it's got location!' says Jo, waving his arm towards the wild, green flatness beyond. 'So we asked the man who has the metal workshop at the top of the lane if he knew anything about the building and this bit of land. He's a really tough-looking bloke, but he looked at us like we're mad and said that he was too afraid to come down here. It's 20 yards from his workshop!'

The sight that greeted them when they ventured to the end of the lane was not a pretty one.

'There were tin sheds where all the sump and waste oils had been stored, but the roofs had collapsed. Water had got in and oil had got out and there was a swimming pool of oil, maybe 100 metres across, in the middle of the yard. And people had been fly-tipping down here, so the oil was trapped by piles of old mattresses, children's toys, bags of clothes...'

'Caravans!' Beth interjects. 'Fridge freezers!'

I look at them both, open-mouthed.

'And those buildings there, where I now have my workshop,' says Jo, 'had had all the copper pipes ripped out for scrap, the windows had all been smashed and there were the remains of fires in the corners where people had been cooking smack.'

'It sounds horrendous.'

'It was. It was a big, big mess. But looking past that mess...' Jo tails off and smiles.

'Jo!' I rub my hands in my eyes in disbelief. 'It sounds like this whole area was just one, big, contaminated fly-tip.'

'That's exactly what it was.'

'And how much did you pay for it?'

'Well, this was the funny thing,' says Beth. 'Jo managed to track down the owner and he said he'd sell it to us for 40 grand. He didn't know that was the exact amount of money we had – we didn't make him an offer, that is just what he said – and he thought the site came with an additional acre of land. It actually has 10 acres, but he didn't care. He'd bought it off someone to help them out. He'd never even been here.'

'And was there anywhere, any of these buildings that you could live in once you'd bought the land?'

'No, we bought that big old static caravan and lived there; and we got some really good pairs of overalls and just started pulling things apart, separating what could be burned, what needed disposing of by specialists. We found a firm to suck away the oil and take all the old fuel that was left in barrels all over the place, but most of it we did ourselves.'

What I still can't quite get my head around is how they had the imagination – and the guts – to believe this site could ever be worthy of the entire content of their bank accounts.

'Jo has the most extraordinary ability to be able to look at things three dimensionally. He can see beyond the surface and the filth, visualize the potential for a landscape, see how to change it and shape it to make it work.'

'It still seems mad.'

'It's a lot less mad than getting a mortgage.'

We're walking now to the garden, down a path planted with willows that they coppice and use for canes and supports for their vegetables. The path enters the marsh and winds through high, rustling reeds on a boardwalk, which they built – of course – from a bridge that was taken down on the other side of the estuary.

'We volunteered to have any of the sleepers that had rot in them and weren't worth reselling. They delivered them for free and we milled them into the boardwalk, so we didn't have to keep trudging through here in our wellies.' From the marsh we come to a paddock where there are lambs that they have hand reared.

'Will you eat them?'

'We will – well, Jo's vegetarian and we don't eat much meat, but yes. We raised pigs last year – really just to rotavate the ground – and we ate them. And shared them with the neighbours. It's a treat when you don't eat meat all the time.'

Around the corner from the paddock we come to a grassy area planted with fruit trees.

'This was just a great, potholed thicket of bracken and brambles,' says Beth. 'This is what I mean about Jo and how he can visualize things and then just do them. And then there's the garden.'

'Wow,' I breathe.

It's a big, level space with a vertical bank of earth at the back and it is full of plants – runner beans, broad beans, sweetcorn, asparagus, squash, potatoes, carrots, beetroot. There are beds of lettuces and herbs, raspberry canes and fruit bushes. 'This was basically a hill,' says Beth. 'We'd had to hire a guy with a digger and a dumper truck to help dig the drains and channel for the cess pipe. He'd leave us the keys at the end of the day and Jo would be in the digger and I'd be in the dumper. We shifted tonnes and tonnes of earth to create the 'wall' at the back to protect the garden from the wind and flatten it out so we could grow as many vegetables as possible.'

'We made all the soil,' says Jo. 'We got garden waste from the council, which then was only £60 for a 10-tonne lorry load, and mixed it with manure from the local stables and sand from the iron foundry. We produce so much stuff, we now run it as a community garden, and we're entirely self-sufficient in fruit and veg from around June to October.

We store lots of it too – we have a Second World War canning machine, dehydrators, juicers, smokers, because it is much more energy efficient to store food that way than in a freezer.'

By now, we have walked around the whole plot and have returned to stand outside the house. It is two storeys high, clad in corrugated iron painted blue, with white windows. Between the ground and first floors, supported by pillars, is a big broad balcony that wraps around the house and looks out over the site and the marsh beyond. On the roof of Jo's adjacent workshop, they've created a terrace, with plants in pots, a big table, loungers and a greenhouse for tomatoes.

We go through the door of the ground floor. The whole space has been dedicated to Beth's studio, where she paints and teaches. Light floods in through big windows, there are easels and tables, stacked canvases and immaculately ordered brushes in jars.

'It was really important for me to have a workspace that is separate from where we live – even though it's the same house,' Beth says. 'So the five of us – our three kids, Pip, Betty and Ruby, and us two – all live upstairs.'

We climb the external metal staircase and enter a generous, high-ceilinged space that is the kitchen, dining and sitting room combined. It is full of books, paintings, mismatched furniture, cushions and rugs, and again, it is filled with light, giving it a sense of grandeur. It is one of the most welcoming rooms I have ever been in. The bedrooms and bathroom are off the corridor beyond.

'And you built all this from scratch?' I ask.

Jo and Beth nod in unison.

'Did you have an architect help draw up plans?'

'No, I drew them myself,' says Jo. 'Beth was six months pregnant with

Betty, our second child, and so I said I'd have the house finished by the time she was born. Or at least something temporary so we could move out of the caravan. But then I got carried away. It took three years to finish, rather than three months, but it was so much fun.'

The slab that the house is built on had to be specially designed because the ground beneath it is unstable, but otherwise they did everything themselves. And neither of them had ever built or helped build a house before.

Even more remarkable is that almost all the materials they used to build the house were second-hand, scavenged or repurposed. The floors are discarded scaffolding boards, the pillars holding up the balcony are from an old church, the kitchen units made from pews. And the actual fabric of the building itself – the insulation and the interior walls – is made from a Fyfe's bananas cold-storage unit.

'It was perfect,' says Beth. 'We had been wondering how we were going to insulate a building of this size. Straw bales seemed the obvious answer, but we couldn't afford even those. Then we were driving past Barry docks and Jo spotted this monstrous pile that had been created when they had pulled down a cold-storage unit and thought: *That would work!* So he went to ask someone about it, who said he'd have to bring it up at the next board meeting. We thought we'd never hear from him again, but a week later he rang us and told us the board had agreed we could have the lot for a fiver!'

'We couldn't afford scaffolding,' continues Jo, 'so we put the first floor in first so we could do the roof from ladders and then we put the panels from the refrigeration unit in, which became the internal walls, ran all the services around the outside of them and then clad the building in tin. So we built it from the inside out.'

'But plumbing? Electrics?'

'We taught ourselves and then asked a building inspector to check and sign them off.'

I look at them both with unabashed admiration.

'And you stuck to your number-one rule?' I say finally. 'You didn't accrue any debt? You did it within your means?'

'We did,' Beth nods. 'Because we had time – we didn't have to go off and work for anyone else, we could be totally committed to this, and we didn't have any pressure. We had no rent or mortgage to pay. When we needed money for something – we couldn't get plumbing or electrical stuff second-hand, for example – I'd teach a few more classes or try and get a portrait commission and it just took as long as it took. And do you know what's lovely? Being able to sit and look around and remember every bit of creating this building, this home. It has given us a unique attachment to it. It's a really, really special feeling.'

The house costs almost nothing to run – they have solar electricity and heating and a woodburner. Jo converted their car to run off vegetable oil, which they buy from the pub opposite for 15p a litre. They grow a big proportion of their food. Their determination to live a debt-free life has forced them to make economic choices that are equally beneficial to the planet. This, although important to them, was not, Beth confesses, at the forefront of their minds when they first started. It is a happy coincidence that what works for them also works for the environment.

We are sitting at their long table. There are bowls of salad from the garden and bread from the local bakery – 'because it's so much nicer than the bread I make!' Our talk has turned to what it means to be rich. Jo and Beth's combined income is between £12,000 and £15,000 a year, significantly less than the minimum wage. And they have three children.

'We don't have money,' says Beth, 'but we have riches. It has helped that we live in such a wasteful society and that we could build a house with stuff people didn't want, furnish it, clothe our children with wonderful cast-offs that may have been worn once or twice before they are passed on. Our fridge and cupboards are full of food, we have a beautiful house, we have great friends and neighbours. We have space, we have time and we don't owe anyone anything. And anyone could do this. It is achievable. It just takes a leap of faith. We are not particularly extraordinary.'

The greatest fruit of self-sufficiency is freedom.
EPICURUS

WHICH WAY NEXT?

*

There are a couple of hours of daylight left and the rain has stopped. I grab my coat, shove my feet into boots, and pull on my woolly hat. Dog and I stride out down the lane, the air cool and damp, the sky still uniformly grey. We turn up the track that will lead us out on to the hill. The route is comfortingly familiar. I know every rock and patch of bog, so my mind wanders, happily flitting between observations and reminiscences, plans and ideas.

I think back, with a little lurch of pride, to the moment when my friend Jo phoned to ask if I would pick up some bread on the way to their house the next day. And I said, 'I'll make you some!' It was Jennifer's black treacle and oat bread, which is simplicity itself, and I now make all the time. I haven't, I am a bit ashamed to admit, felt brave enough to tackle the 'belly of the nun' by myself.

The new year's veg list is drawn up and the seeds ordered. I have stuck, more or less, to my promise to Emma to eschew the exotic and go for no-nonsense, tried-and-tested varieties. Although I did sneak in another black tomato – a different one this time – because I'm determined to grow at least one that is edible. And I'm not going to grow quite as many chillies – but I do want enough to make Amie's chilli jam and Kathy's harissa. My task in the coming weeks (*must order topsoil!*) is to clear the old soil out of the raised beds and, with Ludo's help, rig up some sort of watering system. I'm not aiming for self-sufficiency, just the delicious satisfaction of home-grown veg throughout the summer. Ludo has promised to build a new, bigger cold frame, and I can now help because I have lost my fear of tape measures and power tools.

Which reminds me. I had an email from Miriam. Her Earthship is nearly finished. 'I'll send you photos when it's done. Then you must come and stay!'

I follow the dog along the narrow sheep path that rounds the corner of the hill, revealing the view over the valley to the peaks beyond. I pause here, as I always do, because even on a grey afternoon like this one, it merits a moment just to stand and admire. And as I do, I think of Lundy, and Dean with his great big smile, standing on his wild and windswept rock in the middle of the sea, waiting for his birds to return. And then, of Jo and Beth and their kids, laughing around the kitchen table in their home-made home looking over the great green expanse of the marsh. And, for some reason (I love it when my mind dances like this), of my favourite jumper with the cactus on the front and the three little holes that are now tiny works of art made by me. Oh! I have made a discovery: my local sewing shop offers courses on how to make a patchwork quilt. 'It's a sign!' I laugh. (If you've watched *Sleepless in Seattle* as many times as I have, you'll get that reference.) And it is just the impetus I need to rescue the sewing machine from the depths of the bathroom cupboard (which is still a paradigm of order) and embrace the fear.

We're climbing now, up to the old stone sheep enclosure on the summit. I'm puffing. The dog isn't. She runs ahead and then stops, turns back with a mildly condescending look of sympathy, and I wonder, as I frequently do, whether life would be easier if we had four paws rather than two feet. But life isn't always convenient. And simplicity is not convenience, even though we often confuse the two. Simplicity is not prefabricated; it is not click-to-buy. And you can't just add hot water and stir. To live simply requires a more conscious, more considered state of mind. One that is calm and unhurried and undistracted. And what I've realized is that doing things that the lure of convenience so often robs us of – growing, cooking, making, mending – and taking the time to do those things, is really fulfilling. It brings contentment.

Just a couple of weeks ago, something rather joyful and entirely unexpected happened. Ludo, who has dealt with my clear-outs, my constant weeding, my insistence that things be repaired, with a patient forbearance bordering on saintly, was seized by a sudden desire to clear out my favourite room in the house. The boot room. It is – or rather was – an inglorious chaos of mud, dripping coats, abandoned wellies and the smell of wet dog. Now it has been sorted and swept. New hooks put in walls; hats hung up; a drying rack hanging from the ceiling by a pulley. *And* the light-bulb cupboard, once overflowing with light bulbs dating back to the beginning of the 19th century, now contains only the bulbs we need and each one has been labelled so we know where they go.

'Wow!' I said, somewhat stunned. And then giggled. 'Did you have a light-bulb moment?!'

I got a withering look in return.

Dog and I are standing on the top of our world, at one with the wind and weather, with the soaring kites and scudding clouds. Dusk approaches. We start our meandering descent and I wonder, as I have so often in the last months, why we humans so readily forget our past and what it has taught us. Confucius wrote: 'Life is really simple, but we insist on making it complicated.' And he lived between 551 and 479 BC. Yet here we are, over two thousand years later, still making it complicated. 'The greatest wealth is to live content with little,' wrote Plato (428–348 BC). Why do we regard 'new' as synonymous with 'better'? Turn our backs on old wisdoms? Ignore the experiences of the past? Progress is, in our minds, about moving forwards, but to make real progress, I contemplate, it might be as well to pause sometimes, look back, before continuing to charge ahead.

Dog is charging ahead. It's time for her dinner.

I never did try doing a machine load of washing by hand, I suddenly think. *Sorry, Brenda.*

As we make our way down the final slope, through the heather and the gorse and the wiry winter grass, the evening sun breaks through the cloud on the horizon, flooding the hills and fields with colour and light. And it strikes me that the search for simplicity and contentment starts and ends here: feet firmly on the ground, face upturned to the sky.

> *The Earth is a gem in the cosmos… We have a profound responsibility to care for the Earth, which is our craft on a voyage of both outer and inner discovery.*
>
> EDGAR MITCHELL, ASTRONAUT, *APOLLO 14*

Simple Pleasure #14

— WORKING IN BED —

No sniggering please. Not *that* sort of work. Not at my age. I'm talking about the sort of work you might do at your desk, or at the kitchen table, which can, it turns out, be just as easily done in bed. It was my friend Polly who made this discovery.

'It's marvellous!' she tells me on the phone. 'I'm in bed now.'

I look at the clock on the wall of my office, where I am sitting at my desk, achieving very little. It is 2.15pm.

'I had some really onerous forms to fill in, so I made myself a cup of tea, put a pair of woolly socks on – having warm feet is key – and came upstairs and got into bed. And I think it might be something to do with feeling cosy and cosseted and properly comfortable, in the way that you don't ever do at a desk, that made the form-filling seem less bothersome. So now I'm doing all my writing in bed' – she's in the midst of writing a play – 'and my word count has gone through the roof.'

I have been sitting at my desk since 10 o'clock that morning, working to meet a deadline. I have an article to write, which needs to be sent to my editor by the end of the day. I put the phone down and look at the word count at the bottom of the page on my computer screen. 189 words. I have been commissioned to write 1,500. 'Bollocks!' What have I been doing all this time? There have been the emails that seemed important enough to need dealing with first. Then I attempted to make a start on the writing but couldn't come up with an opening sentence. So I decided to go and make a cup of tea in the hope that it would magically pop into my head. Which does sometimes happen. I got distracted, because we were almost out of milk and everything else – the contents of the fridge amounted to half a sorry-looking lettuce, two carrots and a solitary slice of ham, although there were two bottles of wine. We could, I pondered, as I gazed mournfully into the fridge's bleak interior, share the ham and lettuce and have a carrot and a bottle of wine each. Or I could go shopping. So I made a shopping list. And as I was doing that the postman arrived, who needed something signed for. When I finally got back to my desk, it was almost lunchtime and I still hadn't come up with an opening sentence.

After Polly's phone call, I couldn't get the image out of my head of my lovely, cosy bed just a short flight of stairs away. *Why not?*

I thought, and I unplugged my computer, gathered up my phone, my notebook and pencil case – don't mock, I love my pencil case – and carried them upstairs, feeling that heady mix of guilt and delicious indulgence. I never, not even if I feel like I'm at death's door, take myself to bed in the middle of the day. When people talk about the heavenly prospect of a 'duvet day' – an entire day spent on the sofa or in bed – I can't imagine how they do it. I feel restless and mildly ashamed if I watch two episodes of *Succession* back to back. There are highly acclaimed films that I have avoided going to see because they have running times of more than two hours and I find it almost impossible to sit still for that long. But here I am, getting into bed when it is daylight outside.

The dogs have sensed something untoward is going on, rush up the stairs and jump delightedly on the bed as I'm just settling myself in. I remain fully dressed, which makes me feel less slovenly, and don't get in under the duvet, just the quilt that lies on top of it. But I do have woolly socks on. I arrange the pillows so that I can sit upright and be supported, and I put a pillow on my lap on which to rest my computer. Phone and pencil case go on the bedside table, notebook open beside me. Badger rests his head on my legs, Bella curls herself up on the pillow next to me, Teg stretches out on the floor beside the bed. I start to type. And three hours later I press send. 'Deadline met,' I say to the dogs. 'Let's go and open one of those bottles of wine.'

Not only did working in bed prove productive, it was enjoyable. It felt like a treat. I have resisted doing it all the time, because then it would feel less treat-y, but there are days – particularly if I've got something boring-but-important nagging at me to get done, or the weather is foul and I'm cold – when I happily retreat upstairs and snuggle in.

I'm writing this in bed. There is a tempest raging outside and it's been like that for the last five days. My waterproofs have lost the will to resist the rain any more and I am in a permanent state of dampness. But here I can work, listening to the wind howling around the house, the rain being lashed against the roof and windows, and feel safe and secure and warm. Polly is right though; woolly socks are imperative.

Good night.

*

Some websites you might find useful and/or inspiring:

For lovely off-grid places to stay in the UK and Europe (for a life of temporary simplicity!):
www.canopyandstars.co.uk

For courses in horticulture and more (if you feel your fingers could be greener):
www.schumachercollege.org.uk

For bread-making courses:
www.doughanddaughters.com
(if you are near the Black Mountains in Wales)
www.sourdough.co.uk
(for UK-wide suggestions)

For more information on Repair cafes, including how to set up your own:
www.repaircafe.org/en

To find out more about Earthships or to join the intern programme:
www.earthshipglobal.com

For information on Amsterdam's sustainable floating community:
www.schoonschipamsterdam.org

Camille's sewing courses and workshops:
www.thimblestudios.com

Men's Sheds Association:
www.menssheds.org.uk

Kathy Slack's blog, with recipes and growing tips:
www.glutsandgluttony.com

Lundy Island:
www.nationaltrust.org.uk/lundy
www.landmarktrust.org.uk/
lundyisland

Edventure Frome:
www.edventurefrome.org

Share – the library of things:
www.sharefrome.org

Community Fridges:
www.hubbub.org.uk/the-
community-fridge

Sam Attard's ethical consumer
blog:
www.ethicalrevolution.co.uk

For more information about
artist Beth Marsden:
www.bethmarsden.com

Page 16, *'Fill two tubs...'*
Excerpt from *The Plain Reader:*
Essays on Making a Simple Life,
edited by Scott Savage. Copyright
© The Center for Plain Living,
1998. Reprinted by permission of
The Spieler Agency.

Page 25, 'we started painting...'
'Tirana, Breaking Free from
Communist Past, Is a City
Transformed', by Alex Crevar, *The*
New York Times, 28 August 2015.

Page 99, 'Without hesitation,
the flat-edged...'
Forty-four (44) words from *The*
Craftsman by Richard Sennett
(Allen Lane 2008) (Penguin
Books, 2009) Copyright ©
Richard Sennett, 2008.

Page 121, 'This', he writes,
'has been...'
Excerpts from *Journey*, Mike
Reynolds, 2008. Reprinted with
permission.

Page 127, 'a woman of profound...'
Excerpt from *Remarkable*
Women of Taos, Elizabeth
Cunningham (Nighthawk
Press, 2013). Reprinted with
permission.

Page 130, 'there is a beauty...'
Excerpt from 'What's On Your
Plate?' by Meredith Whitely, in
Washing up is Good for You, Dept
Store of the Mind (Aster, 2017).

Page 193, 'Our project has shown...'
Excerpt from Compassionate Communities UK report reprinted with permission from Dr Helen Kingston.

Page 193, 'a new-fangled innovation...'
'The town that's found a potent cure for illness – community' by George Monbiot, *Guardian*, 21 February 2018.

Page 246, 'I feed the pigeons...'
Lyrics from 'Parklife' reprinted with permission from Blur.

Page 280, 'The Earth is a gem...'
Excerpt from Edgar Mitchell's Foreword to *Voluntary Simplicity*, Second Revised Edition, by Duane Elgin. Copyright © Duane Elgin, 2010. Used by permission of HarperCollins Publishers.

ACKNOWLEDGEMENTS
*

A book needs people to believe in it and having the belief of my agent, Rosemary Scoular of United Agents, and my inspirational publisher, Stephanie Jackson, along with her team at Octopus, is the best start any book can have. Thank you all!

The bones of the idea were given life by the people I talked to and learned from along the way – huge thanks to all of you for your time, expertise, enthusiasm and patience.

Huge gratitude to Caroline MacDonald of The Cottage Company (www.the-cottage-company.co.uk) for finding me the perfect place to hide away and write, and to potter Robin Dale Thomas and Kintsugi artist Yoshi (www.robin-dalethomas.com) for being such kind hosts and providing the inspiration for the book's cover.

When Beth Marsden sent me her first ideas for the illustrations, I loved them instantly. Thank you,Beth, for adding such beauty to the pages of the book.

And to my Wye Valley gang – human and animal – for being there. I'm so lucky to have you.

Kate Humble is a writer, smallholder, campaigner and one of the UK's best-known TV presenters. She started her television career as a researcher, later presenting programmes such as 'Animal Park', 'Springwatch' and 'Autumnwatch', 'Lambing Live', 'Living with Nomads', 'Extreme Wives', 'Back to the Land' and 'A Country Life for Half the Price'. Her last book, *Thinking on My Feet*, was shortlisted for both the Wainwright Prize and the Edward Stanford Travel Memoir of the Year.

www.katehumble.com
🐦 @katehumble
📷 @kmhumble